321- NN
wsb

RELIGION AND THE KNOWLEDGE OF GOD

GUSTAVE WEIGEL, S.J.
ARTHUR G. MADDEN

PRENTICE-HALL, INC., Englewood Cliffs, N.J., 1961

IMPRIMI POTEST

    Joannes M. Daley, S.J.
    Praep. Prov. Marylandiae

NIHIL OBSTAT

    Edward A. Cerny, S.S.
    Censor Librorum

IMPRIMATUR

    ✠ Francis P. Keough, D.D.
    Archbishop of Baltimore
    May 25, 1961

© 1961, BY

PRENTICE-HALL, INC.

ENGLEWOOD CLIFFS, N.J.

LIBRARY OF CONGRESS
CATALOG CARD NO. 62-7448

PRINTED IN THE UNITED STATES OF AMERICA

77319-C

Preface

Religion at all times is a vital concern to man. But, if we may judge from the widespread preoccupation with the subject in the colleges and universities where once it was merely tolerated or ignored and from the number and fine caliber of books being published in the field, religion at the present time has aroused an increased interest and study that goes to its very foundations. This does not mean that in all or even many cases this study has been accompanied by a deepening of the religious spirit or a greater participation in what is called religious activity. The term "religion" is a broad one. It is sometimes used of a concern for the ultimate in the sense of the philosophical absolute implied in all experience. This may be nothing personal but merely whatever one considers to be the ultimate, e.g., matter, idea, nature, and upon which one founds a consistent vision of the universe. On the other hand, religion may refer to the concern with "the holy" as the ultimate ground of being, with that object, transcendent and mysterious, on which all things depend and which we deem worthy of worship. No matter in which sense the term is used, people are concerned.

There are a number of factors in this era which have brought about this increased concern about religion. The catastrophies of two world wars were bound to set many men to examining their ultimate commitments, especially after a century of relative peace and material progress spotted only by localized conflicts. The binding of the nations into one world as a result of these wars and of immense technological progress has made us painfully aware of juxtaposed conflicting visions of the world and of the struggles engendered by them. The challenge within the West of the secular to the Christian vision of the world, the threat to this mixed secular-Christian framework by the Communist faith, the existence of still other visions in the newly rising nations of Asia and Africa, and the clash of all visions in the open arena of world affairs as reflected in the chambers of the United Nations Organization, have left men in a state of confusion and doubt. The confusion and doubt are basic precisely because they are about their fundamental vision of reality. The closer contact with the philosophies and religions of the East has helped to increase this interest in the foundations of religion. The element of mystical experience which is prominent in those religions has caught the attention of the West which for so long has been trying to develop all knowledge along strictly positivist lines. Finally, the ecumenical movements, those embodiments of the desires among Protestants, Orthodox, and Catholics for Christian unity, have led to a reexamination not only of differences of doctrine but also of differences of approach by men to God.

There can be no proper understanding of religion nor can any fruitful dialogue take place among members of different religious faiths unless there is a realization and critique of the premises upon which religious activity is based. Such a philosophical study of religion is the aim of this book. Part I presents a phenomenology of religion and examines the status of religious knowledge. It attempts to answer the question: how can man know God, a reality which is supposed to be so different from the usual objects of our experience that the ordinary categories of our thinking do not fit him? This is what is called the epistemological problem of religion or the problem of our knowledge of God. Part II makes a critical study of one approach to God—the philosophical approach. It concerns the question: what can metaphysics, i.e., philosophy, dictate to man in the field of religion? Can it or can it not provide a rational justification of man's religious activity?

This work is based on courses in religion and metaphysics given by Father Weigel at Fordham University Graduate School. They were part of a cycle of courses in epistemology, religion, and metaphysics presented by him during the years 1950-1956. The editing of the text and the translations from the Greek and Latin writers have been done by Dr. Madden. While this work can stand by itself, underlying its approaches to religion is the general theory of knowledge and the critique of the thought disciplines of science and philosophy treated in another work.[1]

We wish to thank Sister M. Marguerite Andrew R.S.M. and Nancy Waters Neal for their assistance in typing the manuscript, and Mary Nicholson Madden for her part in the proofreading. We wish also to thank those publishers who have so kindly granted us permission to quote from their publications. These are The Macmillan Company, Harvard University Press, Longmans, Green & Company, Inc., and Houghton Mifflin Company, publishers of Riverside Editions.

---

[1] Gustave Weigel and Arthur G. Madden, *Knowledge: Its Values and Limits* (Englewood Cliffs, N.J.: Prentice-Hall, Inc., 1961).

Contents

Eminent theologian and philosopher Gustave Wei-
gel, S.J. (Ph.D. and S.T.D., Gregorian University,
Rome) has lectured extensively both here and
abroad. A prominent author and lecturer, Father
Weigel is Professor of Ecclesiology at Woodstock
College, School of Divinity. His numerous works
include *A Survey of Protestant Theology in Our
Time, Faith and Understanding in America,* and
American Dialogue (with Robert McAfee Brown).
He is the holder of the 1960 Christian Wisdom
Medal awarded by Loyola University of Chicago.

Arthur G. Madden, co-author of the volume, holds
a Ph.D. from Fordham University. A teacher of
many years' experience, he is Chairman of the
Division of Philosophy at Mount Saint Agnes College in Maryland.

Part I

How can man know God?

1

The Religious Phenomenon

The word "religion" is rather elastic and difficult to define in such a way that it will suit all men and be adequately applicable to all the phenomena which men label as religious. Therefore before hazarding a working definition, it would be wise to describe the phenomenon. A grave difficulty in essaying the description of religion is that every man identifies the thing with his own religion—for most men have some kind of religion which they accept even though they may not profess it, or belong to some religious group with a definite theory involved in their religious activity.

Which Groups Shall We Call Religious?

No one will deny that the Christian groups are religious. In like manner Judaism is religious. Moslemism is definitely a religious phenomenon by popular consent, as is Shinto. But after cataloguing the readily admitted religious forms we enter into an area where doubt is possible. Is Buddhism a religion or merely an asceticism involving a religious theory? Is Brahmanism a religion or only a culture based on a philosophy which can be called religious? Most people would consider them religious, but Brahmanism is at its core a pantheism just as Buddha's doctrine is atheistic in appearance.

Then we arrive at the primitive "religions." Is an Indian shaman a priest or a doctor? Is it true as has been said that the Patagonians, who have rites and a code, have no religion? Do the primitives like the Mapuchi or Hottentots merely propitiate earth forces or is there in their ritual a religious element? In some sense primitive legends and rites are considered to be religious. Yet we are faced with the problem whether magic and animism are religious in the proper acceptance of the word.

1

Finally we must consider the ersatz religions. We are told that Communism, which by explicit profession is antagonistic to religion, is a religion. John Dewey and men of the naturalist school wish to develop a religion of humanism which eschews any divinity that is not nature under some aspect or another. Can Science be called the religion of the scientist, or Art the religion of the artist?

What Religion Is Not

We need some concrete observable factor to be able to decide what is phenomenologically a religion. To arrive at it we can do worse than proceed negatively.

The religious *does not consist merely of certain observable actions.*

(1) Ethics is not of itself religion. This is clear in the work of the Greek philosophers and possibly in the work of Confucius. The ethics of Aristotle was in no way a religious exercise on the part of the philosopher. He did not derive his code from anything else but the analysis of human nature without reference to God or something beyond man. Ethics might dictate religious affiliation, but this very fact puts ethics outside of religion and in a way over religion, unless the ethical scheme be derived from religion itself. Morality is quite possible without religious commitments—as is clear in the lives of many self-styled atheists. The morally good man need not be religious, and a man who accepts religious commitments may not be very moral. In Graeco-Roman religion the gods were painted as highly immoral and their cult often took on what was immoral by the ethical code of the people, as for example, the temples of prostitution in honor of Venus.

(2) Socially conducted ritual, symbolic and formal, need not be religious. Many patriotic rituals are definitely not religious, as can be seen in flag ceremonies where heads are bared and dedications made. The Japanese thus understood the worship of the emperor as an act of patriotism and not necessarily a religious worship. During the French Revolution the Robespierrean cult of Reason was definitely anti-religious though there was ritual and cult.

(3) The belief in invisible powers is not necessarily religious. The Mephistopheles of Faust is not a religious object. He is only an earth-spirit. In magic and animism the universe is conceived as a complexus of visible and invisible agents. These agents are not gods but component elements of the world not differing essentially from the grosser material

agents which surround man. If they are not conceived as crassly material, they are at least conceived as subtly material. Magic did not believe in the divinity of the forces it was trying to control; it merely believed that there were secret forces at work in the world in which we live, and that these forces could be controlled by man if he knew the secret. Magic and science agree in principle; they disagree only in their image of the secret forces. Magic personifies; science depersonifies.

(4) Ecstatic states are not necessarily religious. Leuba overlooked this fact in his treatment of the mystical.[1] All states of intoxication are ecstatic, sex experiences are ecstatic, but such states are not religious.

(5) Animism is not of its nature religious, though it believes in a spiritual world. However, these "spirits" are earthbound and earth-marked. The spirits of Chinese ancestor worship, of Spiritualism, are only elements that naturally are tied up with bodies in our ordinary experience. They are not crassly material and when their material compart is dissolved, they retain their identity and their existence. Spiritualism, an abiding phenomenon,[2] is not a religious phenomenon.

From these negative considerations we can come to the conclusion that the *religious* is constituted by something which evades a merely extrovert observation of the religious actions. Nothing that we usually associate with religion is of its structure exclusively religious. Rites, vestments, temples, ethics, and so forth can be non-religious in character.

Can we distinguish the religious by introspection?

(1) Religion is not a peculiar activity by reason of the peculiar structure of the religious act in the light of psychology. Religion is *not an emotion exclusively,* and in as far as it is an emotion, it is not distinguished in structure from other emotions. By emotion we understand the affective tone that accompanies a perception or a conative action, the feeling experienced in other experiences. Religious pleasure is not unique. It is not constituted by something not found in other forms of satisfaction, as, for example, sex pleasure is unique. Religious satisfaction is diffuse and not restricted to the use of one set of organs. Religious satisfaction cannot be distinguished from aesthetic or instinctive satisfaction by reason of the inner structure of the physical act. Hence Matthew Arnold's reduction of religion to ethics and emotion is a most superficial and inadequate summary. Religion can and normally does include ethics and it inevitably produces emotions and feelings, but it is a far cry from saying that it is these things.

---

[1] James H. Leuba, *The Psychology of Religious Mysticism* (London: K. Paul, Trench, Trubner & Co./New York: Harcourt, Brace & Co., 1925).

[2] Cf. I *Samuel* 28, 5-20.

We are told that religion is a *sentiment*. The word can be used loosely as another term for emotion or feeling. If thus understood, we have already dealt with it. If it is used in the sense of some psychologists who by "sentiment" mean a definite constellation of feelings which are proper to psychic states or which correspond to definite objects, then it will be clear that there is a religious sentiment. However, this does not mean that religion is that sentiment, for the simple reason that a sentiment is the consequence of a situation or object. The religious sentiment manifests the religious situation or object, but it does not produce them.

(2) Religion is *not a peculiar mode of perception* or a consciousness other than that which is the matrix of all perception. In its cognitional aspects it uses intuition, experimental knowledge, testimony, reason, and intellection just as any other human concern does. The theologian does not reason differently from his colleagues in philosophy. A consciousness of God is a misnomer, for we are only conscious of ourselves. We can certainly be aware of religious objects, but that awareness is in function of consciousness. The mystical state is a peculiar situation and we shall treat of it elsewhere.

Nor can we recall religion a *mental attitude*. "Attitude" is often defined psychologically as the direction of attention by habit toward a determined class of objects or by the method of a determined mental discipline. Hence there can be and is a religious attitude, but this attitude supposes the religious as prior and is not its constitutive element.

(3) Religion is *not an instinct*. Instinct today is generally understood as a psychic preformation innate in a subject whereby without previous education a set behavior act or pattern, uniform in the species, results from exposure to an apt stimulus. It is something more than an unconditioned reflex which is a simple act of behavior resulting mechanically and not psychically under the influence of the stimulus. Religion is not universal in all men; it seems to require education; its pattern is not uniform. That instincts will come into play in the religious situation is a priori admissible and a posteriori it is evident that they do. However, this does not make religion an instinct.

(4) Religion is *not a faculty*. There is no evidence that men possess a special medium whereby they act religiously. In all religious phenomena all elements can be reduced to the psychic forces at play in all human activity.

Conclusion: Neither by extrovert examination of religious activity nor by introspective analysis do we find in the religious a psychic structure that is peculiarly its own. The determinant element of religious behavior is not structural nor can it be detected by the examination of the structure of religious activity. This activity is most varied. There is religious thinking and perception; there is religious feeling and emotion; there can be muscular religiosity. No class of human action can be excluded from the possible field of religion, and there is no human activity which by structure is exclusively religious.

What Religion Is

Religion is a distinctive human phenomenon. Nothing like it is found off the human plane. If it cannot be determined by the structure of the activities entailed in human activity, it will be determined by something outside those structures to which the structures are related. In other words, the religious is *objective* in tendency. It is an activity *in relation to a certain object, real or supposed.* What is this object? It is the important element in religion, for it alone determines and specifies religious activity.

It is an easy solution to our problem to say that the object is God or the divine. However, this type of solution is not phenomenological unless I can give to the word "God" a phenomenological content. What is more, the word "God" is a fighting word. To some it is a fallacious symbol with no reality attached to it outside of human minds. To others it is an objective reality, but the definitions of such a reality are many. To avoid the acrimonious disputes in philosophy concerning the reality and nature of God, which are metaphysical discussions, let us describe the object of religious action in as far as it manifests itself clearly in the simplest and widest religious actions.

Rudolf Otto in his famous work, *Das Heilige,* calls the object of religion the *numinous*.[3] Now we must avoid the temptation to solve problems by the simple process of giving the unknown factor a name. If a man suffers from a headache, no advance has been made toward his cure by a wise observation that the patient is clearly suffering from an intense cephalalgy. Just because I put the English word "headache" into Greek does not tell me much about the disorder. The mere substitution of the word *numen* for the word "God" has not advanced the discussion. What is more, in Latin, *numen* is a term roughly equivalent to the divine.

Otto himself recognizes that a change of words will not solve the

---

[3] Rudolf Otto, *Das Heilige,* über das Irrationale in der Idee des Göttlichen und sein Verhältnis zum Rationalen, 9 aufl. (Breslau: Trewendt und Gramer, 1922). The English title is; *The Idea of the Holy,* trans. John W. Harvey, revised with additions (London: H. Milford, Oxford University Press, 1926).

problem. He substitutes *numen* for "God" so as to avoid the disputes that such a word will excite. The numinous for Otto has phenomenological content. He understands by it an object on whom the human subject is totally dependent, who (or which) is totally other, and beyond our categories, and who is, in consequence, involved in frightening obscurity, a *mysterium tremendum*, a fascinating, majestic superiority.

It is clear that Otto's description is not philosophical or theological. It is strictly phenomenological. It is valid as far as it goes, though it might be presented differently and better.

Psychologically we can deduce from Otto's description the sentiment proper to this object—the religious sentiment, that constellation of emotions which form the emotional feeling proper to religion. The majesty and obscurity will produce a feeling of awe, wonder, veneration. The note of dependence, utter and complete, on something totally other and tremendous, will induce fear. The fascination will produce love and trust. These four elements—awe, fear, love, and trust—are the component elements of the religious sentiment. It is a highly exhilarating sentiment making the religious experience richly satisfying. Religion is pleasant, even if it were not true.

Evolution of the Numinal Scheme

The last assertion explains an evolution that has taken place over the centuries. In all primitive cultures the numinous is given primacy in life and society. An organized numinal relationship will be constructed and in such a construction magic and animism with their offshoot, fetichism, will enter as component elements. There will be very little theology, though legends and myths will try to unveil the numinous in imaginative symbols. There will be much divination. Society will use the numinous structure for its own needs, and religion in consequence can be an obstacle to modifications and freedom. Some brave spirits will fight the religious. Thus Epicurus, and above all Lucretius, tried to release men from the fear of the gods. They did so with a metaphysic which made all being homogeneous, thus excluding the notion of the totally other, or the numinous. This metaphysic leaned on a naïve epistemology. What you see, is; what you do not see, is not.

The Lucretian attempt to destroy the numinal background of classical thinking failed. However, the religious framework of life was modified by Epicureanism, Stoicism, and Neoplatonism, and was finally transformed totally by Christianity.

Christianity formed the numinal scheme of Europe until the Renaissance when it was attacked by the Humanists, who, however, still were in favor of some numinal conception. The Humanist attack weakened the allegiance of people in lands of Mediterranean cultures (for Catholicism) without erecting an accepted numinal scheme, but in the North of Europe the Reformers substituted a different framework for the hitherto prevailing Catholic one.

The seventeenth century produced the first philosophies which by the eighteenth century produced a new religious movement, that of Deism. Voltaire, Lessing, and the Illuminati in general opposed the numinal scheme on hand and proposed a different one, but they still had no quarrel with religion as such. It was left to the nineteenth century to oppose all religion in the name of materialism, whether it was the naïve kind of Büchner or Moleschott, or the subtler kind of Karl Marx and Auguste Comte. These men wished to destroy all numinal schemes. Marxism is still devoted to this program in theory, though in practice it can make an unstable peace with religion, provided religion submit entirely to the Marxist dictators.

The twentieth century could not hold nineteenth-century materialism because physics soon discovered that matter was not as simple as the nineteenth century had conceived it. There showed up a new materialism, non-reductive, to use the phrase of Roy Sellars. The new materialism took on the name of naturalism, but in its high esteem for values, recognized that religion was pleasant, i.e., had values. They are therefore interested in keeping religion, but they want a numinous that is not totally other or at all mysterious. However, their initial successes were upset by the current trend toward a numinous more in accord with the description of Otto.

2

The Epistemological Problem: Metaphysical Answers

Given the numinous as the object of religion, the problem arises at once: how can the human mind know of its existence and reality? The epistemological problem comes at once on the presentation of the religious phenomenon. Religion is a human reaction to the numinous or God. How does man know God? God is not a reality like the others that man normally knows. He transcends all the categories that man uses to label the objects which impinge on him in everyday experience. Many answers have been given a priori and in the concrete many answers must be given for the individual's assent to the proposition that the numinous is real. The answers that are dictated by a man's vision of *the meaning of reality* must be classed as metaphysical. Many systems that disdain and attack metaphysics are themselves highly metaphysical. Some examples of metaphysical answers, negative and positive, follow.

Negative Answers

The naturalist answer

This is the view of men like John Dewey, Henry Nelson Wieman, Douglas C. Macintosh, Bertrand Russell, and George Santayana. There are naturalists who are opposed to religion and hope to see its demise, but naturalism has many adepts who want a religion quite different from the numinal schemes worked out up to the present. No naturalist can believe in a numen that is totally other. All reality must be fitted into the framework of the cosmos. Nothing is over it; nothing is beyond it. There is in all of these men a faith in the basic univocal homogeneity of the real, which is achievable through experience, controlled by scientific method.

Is the numinous a reality for these men? Not if by the numinous we mean a person or even a being distinct from the cosmos. The personal creator of the Christian and Jewish religions, the intensely personal Allah of the Moslems, cannot be real according to the dogmas of naturalism. Nevertheless for human striving it is necessary to have faith in the possibility in nature to realize values. By this faith man does achieve values and by it human life is enriched. Without such a faith all amelioration would be impossible; in fact, human action would be impossible. Now the potentiality in nature to realize values is there. It is objective and not a human dream. This potentiality is the source of all action in the cosmos, the ground of active being, as all natural beings are. It is the absolute beginning. It is not something distinct from nature but an aspect of it, and the basic value-aspect of it. This is the numinous. This is what is symbolized by the God-legends and the different God-constructs.

Religion is thus a condition for value-pursuits, values always higher and higher. The numinous is the capacity in nature for values; active, original and omnipresent. This is the real meaning of God. The manner of knowing God is nothing but the recognition of capacity in nature for values without limit, a recognition perfectly derivable by the scientific method of experimentation, generalization, and hypothesis.

This description of the numinous is derived from Wieman.[1] In spirit it will reflect the mind of all naturalists who have an interest in religion. Santayana, however, would use Catholic forms, interpreting the dogmas as naturalistic symbols.

Criticism

Leaving to one side the basic metaphysics in this explanation, and ignoring the poverty of an epistemology which will restrict all knowledge to experimental methods committed to nominalism, we can only say that the numinous of naturalism is not numinous. It is of the essence of the numinous as presented by the phenomenon of religion to be totally other; to transcend the order of being which is the connatural object of human knowing. Naturalism denies the possibility of divinity and merely

---

[1] See H. N. Wieman and B. E. Meland, *American Philosophies of Religion* (New York and Chicago: Willet, Clark, 1936), pp. 295-9; H. N. Wieman in D. C. Macintosh, ed., *Religious Realism* (New York: The Macmillan Co., 1931).

uses the language of religion in order to deny the one thing that religion discovers. This borrowed use of language is not treacherous in intent, because naturalists wish to retain the values of religion without the commitments of religion. Atheistic religion is not religion, and it really would be fairer, even though requiring much courage, for naturalists to say that they want no religion but have a substitute for it. The druggist uses this tactic when he tells us he does not have the article we ask for, but he has something just as good.

The atheist answer

This view is not popular in our day. Opposition to this, that, or all religions is common enough, but it is usually justified in the name of religion. The critics want a purer religion than they find. The atheist of the Karl Marx type wants no religion at all, but the very Communists soft-pedal this side of Marxian thought in their presentation of the doctrine to the general public, even an academic public. A naïve materialist must be an atheist, but it is difficult to be a naïve materialist today in the light of the advances of science. Modern materialism is much more subtle; it is "non-reductive." Matter is not inert mass in motion; matter is basically cosmic energy in potency to many expressions. Mechanical energy is only one of these expressions and not all expressions can be reduced to the mechanical. The modern materialist is a naturalist. He will not be an adversary of God, the numinous; but, in the words of Einstein, he believes in the God of Spinoza, the God who is the basis and ground of the real, in the sense that all realities are modes of his being. With this type of numen we have dealt when presenting the naturalistic explanation of man's knowledge of the numinous.

The old materialist had a much simpler solution of man's knowledge of the numinous. He simply denied that there was such a reality, and therefore denied that there could be any knowledge of it. Man's assent to the reality of the numinous is the result of delusion. According to the older positivists, sheer ignorance of reality selected a non-scientific hypothesis of explanation by constructing God. Thus Laplace explained the universe to Napoleon without God, and when asked where God came in, answered, "Nous n'avons pas besoin de cette hypothèse-la." Marx made the numinous the invention of a ruling class in order to keep in subjection the lower classes. Freud saw in the numinous a mere Oedipus-complex projection. In a word, the naïve materialist answers the question, how do we know God or the numinous?, by the simple statement that we do not know the numinous because it does not exist.

It is merely constructed for good or bad motives, though even the best motives are harmful to mankind in its realization of itself.

Criticism

The stark simplicity of naïve materialism is frightening. The numinous has had such an important place in human thought and human life, that great blindness or great audacity is required to throw it overboard altogether. That religions have been and are bad is a proposition that frightens no one, but when we are told that this is so because religion is bad, we shrink. The wisest men of the race have seen in the numinous something real. They have differed in their explanation of this reality, but they did not see their way toward a denial of its reality or reducing it to the state of a mere construct. Men create gods; but man did not create God, for it is hard to see just how gods could be created if there were no knowledge of God. Divinity is a meaningful concept which man achieved because of his experience. Materialism overlooks this experience and solves a problem of great concern by appealing to a metaphysic so adolescent in its pretensions and origins that only an adolescent can be seriously fascinated by it.

The Sartrean formula for the atheistic solution in terms of modern existentialism does not differ in essence from the older answer. Again a metaphysic is postulated, namely that all reality is singular, existent, concrete, totally contingent, circumscribed, active because of anxiety and nausea. Needless to say, this description does not fit the numinous, and therefore there is no numinous. Man has constructed the numinous in order to help himself in his futile anxiety to transcend himself. Once more a metaphysic, with no rational justification, rules out the possibility of the numinous. Sartre is Nietzsche turned pessimist. Nietzsche wished to get rid of God so that man could take his place, while Sartre wishes to get rid of God, so that man need not even be human.

Positive Answers

The answer of the primitives

Primitive people had a very anthropomorphic image of the numinous, but it was a superstructure on an experience. The mysterious aspect of the numen struck them most of all. Concerning its reality they had no doubt nor did they doubt that it was other, but the otherness was in opposition to the experiencing subject as an individual. They did not conceive the otherness as being specifically distinct. They explained the fearful mysteriousness of the numen by an arbitrary desire of the divinity to hide itself, although they recognized that theophanies were frequent. In the mythology of the Greeks and Romans, the gods frequently wandered among men without revealing their identity. In ruder cultures, the divinity would take on the form of animals in order to live among men.

The divinity could be forced to reveal itself.[2] Other revelations were in terms of dream visions, or through the medium of diviners who were under the influence of the divinity either in trance or by inspiration.

Among the primitives the numinous was known by the free revelation of the divinity. These revelations were transmitted to posterity in the form of legend and myth.

In this phenomenon, which we find stretching from Alaska to the German forests, from Japan to the Pacific Islands, we note two things. First, the numinous can be encountered in terms of human experience, though such encounters were not ordinary in the lives of the individuals. The encounter would give rise to an account, and on the basis of the account in terms of faith in the testimony of others, the primitives evolved their religious life. It must, however, be remembered that in their religion they mixed magic, animism, and divination. These three things are not religious phenomena, though they may be confused with religious acts. The primitive is not conspicuously concerned with the numen. His prime concerns are health and prosperity. Magic gave him both and the blank background of magic which only deals with invisible forces gave way to an animistic drop. Most of the objects encountered or believed to be encountered in such rites were earth-spirits, demons, demi-gods. These were definitively attached to the earth and to the tribe. The High God, the true numen, hovers dimly and obscurely over all these superhuman agents. Concerning him little is said or thought.

In summary: the primitive believes in encounter and account as the source of man's knowledge of the numinous. He saw no difficulty in this explanation because it explained all that he knew about the rest of the real. The fundamental difficulty that the otherness of the numen made it beyond human encounter in terms of ordinary human meetings did not vex the primitives too much, though they did recognize it for the theophanies were in dreams, trances, or divine transformations. The other difficulty, namely that testimony concerning the divinity is a different type of testimony than we can find in human affairs, did not annoy the primitive at all. The reason probably is that the primitive knows all he knows in terms of tradition. He is not critical.

---

[2] Cf. Jacob's wrestling with the angel, *Genesis* 32, 25-30.

In a word, the primitive solved the epistemological problem of how we know the numinous by supposing *revelation*, mediate and immediate. This means that God jumps the gap of otherness that separates him from human experience by manifesting himself to some men, and through their testimony to all men.

Criticism

The primitive explanation is valid as far as it goes. It does explain. However, in the explanation there hides a difficulty. The numen being totally other cannot be encountered as he is, for he is separated by otherness. In a primitive theophany the numen took on some material form. In this form, how could it be recognized as the numinous? His simple assertion of the fact would not guarantee the validity of the assertion. God cannot reveal himself, unless the recipient of the revelation already knows him. I cannot believe what God says unless I know there is a God.

Intuitionism

Plato is probably the first to teach that God is intuited by the human spirit. In Plato, however, the doctrine is not clear. It seems that his doctrine of the Ideas as explained in the *Republic* supposes that by asceticism man can rise from a consideration of material things to the intellectual forms of material things and from intellectual forms as specifically realized in matter one can rise to the intuition of more general forms with no specific realization until one reaches the highest of all forms which is the Supreme Good or God. His route seems to be: sense objects, specific forms, forms of generic realization (ta mathematica), transcendent forms, the absolute good.

Plotinus certainly thought that this was Plato's doctrine, and the mystical experience, the direct perception of the highest, was for him the natural goal of human thinking. This Neo-Platonism certainly influenced Christian thinking from Augustine to our time, and it is the basis of all Christian mystical thinking.

In a slightly different form this theory seems to be the essence of *yoga* and *Buddhism*. For the yogi and the Buddhist in his search for Nirvana, the goal of all his asceticism is the moment when he can see the numinous face to face. The Buddhist in his fidelity to the notion that the numinous is totally other claims that the last stage is entrance into nothing, but does he not mean probably the entrance into the level of the no-thing, i.e., reality transcending our category-catalogue?

Something of this doctrine is universal to all peoples. In *Hebrew religion* Yahweh is known through revelation, but the medium of the revelation at the high point of his mission sees God as God, but only the "back parts." (*Exodus* 33, 17-23). In all peoples there is always the tradition that there were men among them, great seers (see-ers) who not only witnessed a theophany, but actually saw God. No attempt is made to explain the how of this event. The traditions are content with the narration of the event as true.

Joseph Maréchal gives us the account of the passion and death of al-Hallaj, the Moslem mystic, which is a tradition of Islam, where again we have the man who sees the numinous in itself.[3]

Ontologism. The previous forms of intuitionism were strictly mystical, i.e., an ecstatic and unusual form of intuition of the numen. However, an intuition of the numinous which is not ecstatic but rather implicit in all knowledge has been taught over and over again. Pascal had some kind of ontologistic approach to God. The German mystics before him, Meister Eckart and Heinrich Seuse, developed an epistemology which posits a non-ecstatic intuition of the Absolute as the origin of knowledge in general and in every instance.

However, the word "ontologism" was applied to the doctrines of two Italians of the nineteenth century, Gioberti and Rosmini, ardent Catholics, who wished to begin philosophy with a recognition of the absolute in the intuition of being as such. For them *being as such* and the numinous were synonyms. The ontological recognition of being was not a mystical encounter with God. It was no rapture. It was, of course, non-rational, in the sense that it was not the conclusion of an inference. Rather it was a condition for knowledge and was always the first element in knowledge. This intuition was intellectual and not a voluntaristic thrust.

Dialectical Ontologism. Karl Barth is vehemently against any rationalistic approach to the numinous. His formula is that the numinous, God, reveals Himself as Lord and Savior, in vital encounter. The man who has best developed this thought, though he is not at all a Barthian, is Paul Tillich, formerly of the Union Theological Seminary in New York, now at Harvard Divinity School. For him the numinous comes to man freely, i.e., there is no determination of nature that will make man meet God. However, God is the ground of all being and is therefore the

---

[3] Cf. Joseph Maréchal, *Studies in the Psychology of the Mystics,* trans. Algar Thorold (London: Burns, Oates and Washbourne, 1927), Sec. v, "The Problem of Mystical Grace in Islam."

prius[4] of all thought. He is not contained in thought conceptually but is encountered as the ground of human concern in every human decision and judgment. The note that Tillich strikes hardest is that the numinous is an object of vital concern, something that requires man's total submission. It cannot be expressed in concepts; it is not the conclusion of an inference; it is the anxious recognition of man's finitude and the dangers of any choice that throw man against the limits of his being with anxiety, and these limits touch the fuller reality that surrounds man and supports him. For Tillich it is useless to apply reason to this reality; it is given in experience, and it is accepted in trust and faith. It is God revealing himself, not through words and concepts, but in vital encounter in terms of human anguish and incompleteness. For Tillich there can be no atheist, because every man receives the revelation of God inasmuch as man is constantly thrown up against the limits of his own being, and thus thrust upon God who bounds him in. So-called atheists only revolt against inadequate formulas of God which reduce him to the category of things in finite nature. God is beyond these categories, and to force him into categories is idolatry. This for Tillich is the great sin to which all organized religions are tempted. They identify the ineffable numen with something finite, or raise the finite, the imperfect to the order of the transcendent numen.[5]

Criticism

As has been clear from the rapid exposition of intuitionism, there are three basic forms of it: mystical, non-ecstatic intellectual, non-ecstatic voluntaristic. Concerning the mystical we shall say nothing here. Mysticism is a phenomenon of religion, perhaps the high phenomenon, but it is not the current experience of men in religion. Let us stick to the phenomenon as the vast majority of men know it. The intellectualistic form of intuitionism as developed by Gioberti and Rosmini is justified by the identification of being with God. That all men have an intuition of being is clear enough, for otherwise they could make no judgment whose dynamic element is the verb "to be." In terms of being all judgments, even the first, are made.

However, it does not seem to be true that being as the quasi-concept in all human assertion is synonymous with divine. If it were, then every

---

[4] *prius*—that which is prior or basic; hence, the pre-condition of thought.
[5] Cf. Paul Tillich, *The Protestant Era* (Chicago: University of Chicago Press, 1948); also Gustave Weigel, S.J., "Paul Tillich and Contemporaneous Protestantism" in *Theological Studies* (June, 1950).

being would be divine, and the otherness of the numinous would disappear. Even pantheism, which makes such a statement, is careful to
give otherness to the numinous, though this care seems to be nullified
from the outset. It is true that a metaphysical analysis will show that
being must have divine roots, but this is a far cry from saying that being
of itself is divine. Stones are. Men are. Thoughts are. Yet these things
are not the numinous. Nor can we say that the numinous cloaks itself in
these forms, for we predicate being of these objects without any commitment to divine reality.

It seems to be true that being *virtually* says God, by reason of metaphysical implications which are recognized clearly after a metaphysical
reflection. However, a sheerly psychological reflection finds no divinity
in being, except when we are dealing with the numinous real. Intellectual
ontologists confuse the metaphysical reflection with the psychological
reflection. Saint Thomas saw clearly that: omnis affirmatio est implicita
affirmatio Dei,[6] but he also saw that this did not mean that we have an
implicit intuition of God. Existent reality is first achieved as existent
reality with no concomitant realization of the truth of God. Metaphysics
can show that no reality can be such unless related to the absolute which
is God, but such a metaphysical meditation is a new insight gained after
some spontaneous recognition of the real in any form. The new insight
must not be attributed to the older insight, nor is it a phenomenological
element of the previous experience. Being does not *formally* say divinity,
though it can when referred to the numinous.

The intellectualistic ontologist in his fervor to justify his adhesion
to the reality of the numinous makes too hasty an analysis of the religious
phenomenon.

The voluntaristic ontologist wills God to be. This, unfortunately, is
not a safe process. Man wills many things, but as his will is not creative,
he cannot give reality to the willed in every case. Tillich has diluted
the voluntarism of dialectical theology with much intellectualism. However, he stands and falls on one supposition: the recognition of limitation
is simultaneously the recognition of the unlimited which surrounds the
limited. Attention to the contained does not bring with it an awareness
of the container, though by reflection an insight of the container is possible—but it was not given in the first awareness as a component element
of awareness. The second insight is in function of metaphysical thinking,
and the whole purpose of the Tillich approach to God is to eliminate
metaphysics and reason from the encounter. Tillich stresses too much
the otherness of the numinous. If the numinous is too utterly other, he

---

[6] Every affirmation is an implicit affirmation of God.

cannot be grasped at all. Some continuity must exist with reality on the numinous level and reality on our level. If there is an unbridgeable gap, no one can cross it, and if there is a bridge, there must be points of support, homogeneous in some sense, on both sides. If man is the image of God, then there is in God something of man. He cannot be inconceivable other. That our categories are constructed to deal with the finite is clear enough, but is it true to say that they cannot be used in analogous fashion for the infinite? If they cannot, how can we know the numinous at all, for we must know him with the only instruments at our disposal, categories and class-concepts. The voluntaristic ontologists simply cannot speak of God at all, and yet they do speak of him and they wish to speak of him, and in so doing they use categories and class-concepts. In strict logic they must admit that they are talking non-sense, because the divine for them cannot be expressed by these things.

All dialectical thinkers have an answer to this difficulty by reason of their understanding of semantic expression. The proposition does not carry meaning; it merely is a pointer which stimulates the hearer to experience. Even with this doctrine the original difficulty is not met. We think that the principle of Kant, sensations without concepts are blind, is valid. If it is valid, then experience itself supposes conceptualization as an element in a meaningful act of knowledge. If this is true, then even in encounter the divine is met through concepts, and not immediately. That there can be conceptless experience of God should be granted, but an appeal to such an experience is an appeal to mysticism, and the Tillich doctrine does not wish to be mystical.

Rationalist verification of the numinous

Saint Thomas and his followers justify the knowledge of the numinous through reasoned reflection on reality. The famous "five ways" of the first part of the *Summa,* analyze reality as we meet it and through the analysis see the relation that connects the finite with the infinite. There is no experience of God, but there is proof of his existence. We do not meet him directly, but he is attached to everything that we meet. He is the other side of the moon which we never see, but which we know is there.

The Catholic Church has made this position her own. The Vatican Council insists that so is God knowable.[7] The recent encyclical, *Humani Generis,* repeats this doctrine and insists upon it. This method of knowing the existence of the numinous has been the apologetic and preamble toward faith in Catholic thought throughout the centuries, and especially

---

[7] Conc. Vat. sess. iii, cap. 2, DB 1785.

so in the defense of the numinous since the empiricist attack on the capacities of reason from Thomas Hobbes on. Protestants used this argument, and Theodicy is a Leibnizian creation.

The simplest form of the argument is the one from Saint Paul. (*Romans* I, 20.) The invisible structure of the divinity is seen by men through the understanding of what he has produced. This is an appeal to the principle of causality. On analyzing the five ways of Saint Thomas, it is evident that the most basic form of the argument is that the relative demands the existence of the Absolute.

Criticism

This mode of achieving the Absolute has been under attack for a long time. In the Middle Ages there were movements that did not relish this approach. The Victorines and the German Theology of the fourteenth century did not attack it, but they preferred a road of encounter. The argument was strong among the Deists who in fact accepted it because the faith of Europe in the principle of causality was firm. The Humean attack and the Kantian criticism made the principle of causality suspect, and it was the mode of the late nineteenth century to dismiss the use of the principle as invalid.

William James expressed the modern opposition to the arguments. He proposes the whole natural theology position which he summarizes admirably, only to show that it is not to the point.[8]

The dynamism of William James' opposition to the rationalist approach to the numinous is his distrust of intellection. He is a voluntarist, and he believes that we achieve our goals by thrusts of the will rather than by intellectual perceptions. At the midpoint of the twentieth century this prejudice is widespread, and the Catholic thinkers in Germany and France were exposed to its contagious influence as the encyclical, *Humani Generis,* shows.

The strong point in the voluntaristic position is that the intellectualistic approach to God is a post-factum rationalization rather than a road to the numinous. The voluntarist says that nobody ever came to be religious by the study of the proofs of the existence of God, and that the arguments can only be accepted by believers who acquired their belief some other way. Consequently the reasons for the existence of God are dialectical play; they are useless for non-believers and believers alike. Voluntarists, whether they be Pragmatists or Existentialists, look for other ways of coming to know God.

---

[8] Cf. William James, *Varieties of Religious Experience* (New York: Longmans, Green & Co., Inc., 14th impression, 1907) Lecture XVIII, pp. 433 ff.

The weakness of the critics of the rational achievement of the numinous is their supposition that the metaphysical arguments for the reality of the numinous are a road to conversion. This has never been the burden of those who propose the arguments, with the exception of the eighteenth-century Deists. Neither Saint Thomas nor Catholic tradition believe that conversion, i.e., the recognition of divinity, will take place through the exclusive use of metaphysics. There is a legitimate place for volitional thrust, and even intellectually the proofs, though sufficient, are not enough to move the vast majority of people. According to Catholic views, it is morally necessary that God himself reveal his being in order to avoid errors in man's understanding of God. This revelation works according to principles quite different and superior to the principles of mere reason, though it does not contradict reason. The Catholic doctrine would quite willingly grant the truth of the voluntaristic observation that men do not come to God by syllogisms. It was Saint Ambrose who said, "Non in dialectica complacuit Deo salvum facere populum suum." However, the Catholic position merely insists that if we do not reach God through syllogisms, yet we cannot reach him without the syllogisms. The syllogisms are conditions for meeting God validly, though they are not necessarily the cause.

What voluntarists do not see and cannot see because of their anti-intellectualism is that the intellectualist simply must adopt a position similar to that of the Catholics. The voluntarist does not *know* that he has reached the numinous. He simply *trusts* that he has, and the more vital the trust, the securer he *feels*. However, feeling and trust are such weak supports in an objective world which is what it is quite independently of our feelings and trusts. The intellectualist is right in demanding the confirmation of trust by the real, and only the intellect achieves the real luminously. There is no objection from the intellectualist's viewpoint that there be thrusts toward God in terms of voluntaristic dynamism. He merely wants to see that these thrusts are not into a void. The invisible numinous must be simultaneously achieved not only by feeling and trust but by intellectual assimilation, and in the case of the invisible, only reason through its recognition of relationships, which is an indirect acquisition of the relatum, can make secure the feeling-approach toward divinity. The stubborn insistence of Catholicism that God can and must be known by reason itself is salutary, for only in this way can we be validly sure that the numinous is there, even though the numinous be active with the subject before the subject's reflection on the rational grounds for accepting the numinous. When the acceptance is made, it includes with logical priority the rational conviction that the numinous is real. A rational conviction is possible to anyone, even those who know nothing of logic, be it that of Aristotle or anybody else. Logicians did not invent reasoning; they only proposed controllable methods for its use.

Supernatural revelation of the numinous

This mode of apprehending the numinous is the Catholic solution. The basis of this theory is that by faith, i.e., assent because of testimony, a man reaches the numinous. As we have seen, in order to make this faith reasonable there is required as a logically anterior act, even though temporally it be simultaneous, a ratiocination whereby by pure reason the reality of the numinous be recognized.

This faith is acceptance of truth on testimony. In generic nature it is no different from the kind of faith we give to most of the truths we know. That we are the children of the people who claim to be our parents is an act of faith. That there was a war in Korea is an act of faith. That Mr. Kennedy is the president of the United States is an act of faith. This faith is so easy that it is a sign of mental disturbance when such objects of faith are denied. By the principles of reason it cannot be proved by sheer analysis that there was a war in Korea. The overwhelming majority of humanity had no experience of the war in Korea. Only by faith, the acceptance of the testimony of others, can we know the fact.

Religious faith, as the Catholic understands it, is like this human faith but also unlike it. The revealing divinity must meet history in some man or men in personal encounter. This encounter requires a modification of the perceptive powers of the person involved in the encounter. His intellectual powers must be augmented and raised to a higher plane of activity, and by this reason faith is supernatural. The person can recount what he has experienced, and a third person can now put an act of faith in the account, but even he must be modified interiorly. His intellect must be supernaturally fortified. Given this fortification and given the recognition in terms of arguments valid by natural logic that the account is what it claims to be, a message from the numinous, the individual then can know the divinity. Orthodox Protestantism is not essentially different in its justification of religious knowledge. The only difference is that Protestants make the achievement of God the personal encounter of divinity through the stimulus of a set of books called the Scriptures. By a modification of the perceptive powers of the reader or listener, he is capable of achieving God luminously. However, orthodox Protestants are inclined to be negligent of rational confirmation of the act of knowing through a reasoned conviction of the existence of God and a reasonable verification of the authenticity of the organ of revelation, the Bible. Liberal Protestants and Dialectical Protestants reduce faith to a feeling and trust, overwhelming by its presence without any preoccupation for the possibility of rational justification whose possibility they generally deny. In Judaism and Islam we also have the theory of revelation, but Jewish and Moslem thinkers do not seem to be too interested in the explanation of faith and revelation, and in general we would not be unwarranted in saying that they take the primitive view of it.

The Catholic theory is hardly simple. It is complicated but not confused. Let us examine it with reference to the three moments that it postulates.

The preparation

Before the human agent can meet the divine as divine, he must be prepared. The pure reason is by structure and function quite capable to reason to the existence of God, but the fruit of such reasoning is very meager, and given the human mind as we find it now, it is morally impossible for it to move securely by mere natural ratiocination.

Since the divine is the creator, it lies in its power to direct the existence of men along certain paths. A need for God will be engendered through various ways; generically, it will be a discontent with reality as experienced by the subject. Guilt, suffering, disappointment, trials, the incompleteness of the finite, all can draw the attention of the human being toward a horizon beyond the finite, though it remains only the horizon of the finite itself. There is therefore an external push on man toward the question of God. There is also an internal push within the intellect and will. In both, the basic drive toward fullness is directed toward the inevitable limitations of everything cosmic. In his poem, "The Hound of Heaven," Francis Thompson shows such a preparation. Nature as experienced by the poet was not a mother but only a stepmother. Human love was not as satisfying as the poet had wished. Science leaves so many question marks.

In this preparatory stage the revelation made to mankind and still abiding in the testimony of human monuments and institutions is met as another facet of experience. Its mere presence will not draw the observer efficaciously, but it has a drawing power in terms of man's hope for satisfaction. The greater the feeling of dissatisfaction with the cosmos, the greater will be the drawing power of the revelation as an historic fact. In this stage a man may reflexly reason to the existence of the Absolute. He may do so spontaneously and implicitly. He may not do it at all.

The encounter

Given the preparation achieved in the plan of the Deity, there comes a moment when a new light is lit in the intellect of a man. This light is not natural to man. It is a free gift of the numinous. The intellect under the influence of a will pushing forward toward the great good, a push not natural to it but thrust into it by God, directs its light on the revelation. The revelation now becomes luminous and is humanly acceptable as the manifestation of God. Simultaneously there is a recognition in terms of logical processes that the revelation can be safely accepted as such according to the norms of testimony in things human. This recognition of itself needs no grace, though grace universally acts to make the recognition humanly possible in terms of volitional thrusts and obstacles. Prior to this recognition there is an assent to the reality of the numinous because of a reasoned analysis of finite life. This recognition may have taken place in the stage of preparation, or may take place in the first instance of encounter, but it must take place. For this recognition no divine elevation of the intellect is required, though divine direction of attention and divine orientation of existence will expose the agent to the volitional stimuli favorable to the will's beneficial influence on the intellect. This influence will be exercised by turning the intellect toward the numinous relatum beyond the finite. The last action of the human being is the acceptance of the revelation as true because God is the testifying revealer. Knowledge of the numinous is achieved but as faith and not as vision or as inference.

The three points of encounter must be put into clear relief.

A reasoned assent to the reality of the numinous. This may be temporally prior to the acceptance of the content of the revelation, or it may be temporally simultaneous. However, it is always logically prior.

A recognition that it is humanly prudent to consider the revelation to be what it claims to be: a divine element in history manifesting God to men through divine affirmation. An elevating influence on the intellect is not strictly necessary, but given the confused human mind some help will be given to it by God in order that it make this discovery. Such a help could be merely the direction of attention of the intellect in terms of divine governance of reality.

This point in the faith-encounter is realized in different fashions by different human beings. The early Christians did not make long investigations into the historical events which were narrated by the first missionaries. The experienced joy of acceptance was sufficient warrant for them. Children achieve their credibility of the revelation as they achieve most facts; by simple trust in the words of their elders. Many men achieve it through pragmatism—the assumption that a given revelation is authentic if it works. This pragmatic verification is sufficient. Not much history is studied.

An acceptance because of divine testimony of the content of the historical revelation as illuminated by the light inserted by God into the intellect. Now the numinous is known with detail and with the full numinous overtones, but the knowledge is not vision but warranted belief.

For this acceptance the numinous broke through the wall of otherness three times: (1) when he spoke to the prophet, i.e., mouth-piece; (2) when he gave to the prophet non-natural powers of intellect to understand the speaking as divine; (3) when he impregnated the intellect and will of the believer with new force in order to be able to meet the numinous in faith. This impregnation may take the form of an abiding power, called by Catholic theology the habit of faith, which, since it is always there, needs only the divinely given stimulus to work. So infants have faith after Baptism—not as an act but as a habit.

The reflection

The encounter need not be violent. It need not be emotionally tense. It can be any of these things, just as need not be. However, the encounter is a passing phenomenon in a human being working with concepts on problems of concern. The vestiges of the encounter abide in memory; the commitments made abide in the will. These things affect action and thought. By reflection on the encounter the believer can orientate his actions or consider the structure of the numinous or faith.

In such a reflection there is more than a philosophical analysis of a phenomenological kind; the very content of the revelation is also used as guide for the understanding. The brilliant object illumines itself to permit a photographic grasp of it.

In the reflection we find the believer always guided by the revelation itself. He cannot prescind from it, except methodologically. By method he may not formally consider the data of revelation, but as a human being he does.

As said before, Orthodox, Protestants, and Moslems could use this theory. They rarely do, because they have a deep distrust of intellectualization. Protestants of the liberal variety simply deny that there is any rational justification for the whole event; that it is valuable is justification enough. The orthodox Protestant admits there is a rational justification but he is not much concerned with it. He gives much importance to the experience as imperious by itself. The dialectical theologians have made this importance exclusive. However, on principle they are not committed to their stands. They all differ from Catholics not on the question of faith, but on the vehicle of revelation. For Protestants of all shades, the vehicle is the Bible, illuminated by God for the individual reader. For Catholics the carrier of revelation is the Community called the Church, with an organ of authentic definition. The teaching of the Church takes on many forms: authentic declarations, Bible propositions, liturgical symbols, theological consensus, Church law, Catholic piety and conduct. The carrier of revelation, the Church, is essentially a living thing which is a human society shot through with divinity as an abiding inner principle.

Implicits in the Catholic position

The Catholic scheme of explaining the knowledge of the numinous contains many propositions implicitly.

(1) There is an insistence that human reason as such, without any intrinsic elevation is capable and prone to discover the numinous. No transformation by grace is required, though some kind of grace may be in play, but perhaps no greater grace than the direction of attention to the horizons of finitude on the part of the creator-governor of all action in the universe.

According to the Catholic theory, the discovery is both of the existence of the numinous and also of its nature in broad outline. Now although Catholicism insists on this capacity of the intellect, and though the insistence is the cause of scandal to others, yet in religious life Catholicism does not lay much stress on this rational discovery of the numinous. The reason for this is that by means of reasoning I do not meet God in encounter but rather I know the necessity of his existence. I do not meet him; I only know that he must be there. In my analysis of this necessity I can say something of his nature, but it will be expressed by concepts whose primary function is to describe and understand the finite. The result is that reason gives me not so much a numen as a philosophical absolute, with a blurred face, so blurred that it is almost faceless. It certainly cannot be the object of prayer, that great act of religion, which is possible when the "it" of reasoned achievement of the *necessity* of its being, rather than of its being, turns into the "thou" of human encounter. It is humanly impossible to be devoted to the Prime Mover. In fact, in Aristotle, the father of the Prime Mover notion, there was no religious relation of man to the Prime Mover.

The God of reason is a matter of philosophical orientation and not a matter of human commitment.

(2) The achievement of the numinous as numinous, i.e., as more than a philosophic absolute, is a supernatural act. This derives from the otherness of the numinous. The otherness must not be exaggerated out of all meaning, but it must at least mean that the restrictions of nature do not apply to God, and that the concepts which are adequate for natural things must not be used of God univocally. The knowledge of God as numinous, i.e., in himself by encounter, must be off the natural plane of action.

This position commits the Catholic to the belief of reality beyond the cosmic structure, and makes naturalism the necessary adversary of Catholic thought and aspirations. It also commits the Catholic to believe: (a) that man is capable of supernatural action and being, provided this capacity be called into act by God—nothing in nature could call it forth; (b) that there is a continuous spectrum of reality, even though there are different wave-bands of it. This continuity shot through with discreteness is the famous notion of the analogy of being. The word "is" can describe different levels of being truthfully, but it never has the same content *in toto* for beings on different levels. God is totally other, but with the otherness of being, not with the otherness that excludes him from being.

These two propositions—(a) there is in man an obediential potency for supernatural action, and (b) being is necessarily an analogous quasi-concept—are fundamental to Catholic philosophy. They cannot be tampered with, much less eliminated.

(3) Although Catholicism is stoutly intellectualist, it does not overlook those facts which are stressed by voluntarism. (a) Catholicism insists on the free gift of revelation, the contingence of the giving of the numinous. No matter what be man's preparation for the divine encounter, it depends on God to grant the encounter for no other motive than because he wants to. The revelational break-through was free and the illumination by grace to see and grasp the content of the message given in the break-through are free actions on the part of God. There is no inevitability of it. Reason cannot detect any law of universality for revealing action. What is more, Catholicism insists that the Preparation, all of whose actions are on the natural plane of activity, is a divine intervention, not necessarily in terms of elevation but at least in terms of divine governance toward this end. (b) Catholicism insists that the acceptance of revelation is a free action on the part of the human believer. It requires choice and decision; it is not a forced natural act. All choice and decision carry with them anxiety and free commitment. Faith will not be different. There is none of the repose of the "nothing-can-be-done-about-it" reflec-

tion of necessary action. (c) Catholicism insists that will-forces lead the believer to his faith. He never *sees* the object of his assent. He takes it on authority, and the moving force is the goodness of such acceptance. Intellect can only show that it is reasonable, but not that it is reasoned. Saint Thomas teaches that there is a connatural push in the will to lead the intellect to God. Will and intellect cooperate always. Rationalism, which teaches that all intellectual assent is achieved in terms of the analysis of self-evident principles of thought, is just as much an adversary as naturalism and voluntarism.

(4) Catholicism is committed to a wide metaphysics. (a) With the naturalist it admits that there is a natural order which is the proper background of man. Against him, it refuses to limit reality to this order, admitting a reality beyond it and the possibility of man acting in the higher order, given a divine elevation. (b) With the rationalist it admits that truth can be achieved by using the self-evident principles of reason, which are only the expressions of basic intuitions of the human mind. Against him, it refuses to reduce all knowledge to this kind and admits that experience can bring knowledge unattainable to rationalism. (c) With the idealist it admits that reality is primarily spiritual, i.e., of the stuff that thought is made of. Against him, it refuses to reduce all reality to spirit, admitting that there is a material level of reality, achievable by thought but of a structure distinct and independent of thought. (d) With the empiricist it admits that experience brings with it thinking, but against him it refuses to restrict all thought to empirical objects. (e) With the voluntarist it admits that basic pushes in man lead even his thinking, but against him, it refuses to say that all thought is nothing but voluntaristic subjectivism. Will moves the intellect to being, and in the light of that achievement refines and defines its own pursuit. (f) With the existentialist, it admits that man is contingent and subject to free play of forces, but against him, it refuses to say that this contingence is pure contingence, but rather direction from a free creator himself necessary, wise and good.

This polar type of thinking, characteristic of Catholicism in all its history, is most impressive. It also means that there is a tension in Catholic thought, a refusal to be drawn by one pole and an energetic striving to keep in the counteractive field of the other pole. Tension always means energetic striving. To achieve balance of forces requires great effort on the part of the tightrope walker. Yet the result is grace, achievement, and liberation.

The polarity of Catholic thought must always make Catholicism unpopular. At any moment, usually in reaction to the opinative climate of a previous age, people swing to one pole, losing the attraction of the other. The Church's deliberate fidelity to the other pole will be considered as willful treason and she will be criticized and attacked for her seeming treason. As the ball of opinion swings back it will reach a position identical with the Catholic one, but with a tremendous difference. The swing is to the other pole and the moment of identity is planned to be passed, so that even when identity is momentarily reached, there is no love for Catholicism since it is known beforehand that she will not relinquish the middle position. When she defends liberty against tyranny, non-Catholics will not be convinced. When she defends objective order against arbitrary arrangement in the name of liberty, she will be accused of reaction. When she defends reason against anti-intellectualism, no rationalist is satisfied because he knows she also defends contingency against absolute determinism. It is no easy task to defend equilibrium, and children prefer to sit on the ends of the teeter-totter rather than at the dead center.

General Conclusions

The question: metaphysically how can the numinous be known?

The narrower the metaphysics of the philosopher, the narrower will be the response of the philosopher to the problem of religious knowledge. The crux of the problem is the otherness of the numinous. Any philosophy that reduces that otherness to a specious otherness, simply must reject the numinous even though there is a verbal acceptance. Materialism, naturalism, and idealism insist that being is homogeneous and that consequently there can be no otherness within being. Naturalism must make God some aspect of nature, and of course this makes him cease to be God. Idealism makes of God the ultimate subject of thought, either as the sum total of all thought whereby it can be a cohesive substance as in Hegelianism, permitting circles of thought within one large all embracing circle, or as the subsisting thought at the center with dependent thoughts projected by it to a periphery as finite modes of the infinite center. In any such scheme, reality, being thought, is one in substance, but many in modes, which are still one with the basic substance. There is no true otherness. Voluntarism refuses to the intellect any capacity for achieving the real, which is the blind object of a blind will, which uses thinking blindly as an instrument of acquisition. There is no real meaning to God in this scheme, because there is no real meaning in the cosmos; there is only value, and God is reduced to the value of a finite being. The broader the metaphysics of the thinker, the broader is the possibility of his explanation of the knowledge of the numinous. In Catholicism there is a supernatural answer in terms of a free action on the party of the deity, unpredictable and freely determined by him alone. Yet this explanation supposes the basic discovery of the absolute in philosophy, a discovery not only possible to all men, but which *de facto* is made by all men with different degrees of purity of discovery.

Whereas some philosophies permit only a mystical conquest of God, Catholicism, though admitting this, also insists that there is a rational conquest as well, and also an acquisition by faith.

Excursus on the analogy of being

Metaphysics deals with being, and no thinker can refuse to make some kind of commitment concerning being.

A nominalist can consider being as a label of indefinite extension to cover all possible objects of experience. The word is thus the ultimate class of all classes. It has only extension, no comprehension; and the extension is indefinite because it excludes nothing that can be subject to a synthesis of an organization for rational discussion.

A realist of the naturalistic, materialistic, or idealistic persuasions makes of being a construct-concept with comprehension so that all objects in the extension univocally say the same comprehension, e.g., "Being is thought stuff"; "Being is the correspondent of empirical perception."

An analytic realist will make of being a quasi-concept to correspond to the intuition that being is basic to a reality, but realities are not univocal in their realization of being, e.g., a triangle is a figure of three sides; John is tired. Being is equal to being in diverse realities, but not identical. This equality is not the sign of identity either in thought or reality but only a sign of capacity of being labeled by the same form, or better, quasi-form. This equality in beings is not of one being to the other being, but to the relationships involved in the beings. *It is an equality of proportionality*. The image is taken from algebra. 2/4 equals 4/8. There is here no identity, because two beings are involved in the equation. There is only equality; the same form of reality is manifested in two beings. Even the equality is not of thing with thing, but of relations with relations. The 2/4 relationship is equal to the 4/8 relationship, and this is made evident in terms of the reduction to 1/2.

Now for a being to be such, two things are required of it: (1) it must be distinct from all other things; (2) it must have its proper meaning. It must have *Sosein* and *Dasein,*[9] essence and existence. Where the existence is only the existence of thought, the being is ideal. Where the existence is extramental, the being is actual. All essences by concept have existence potentially and will necessarily have ideal existence in the mind of God. In themselves they have potential existence, which is enough to give them the reality of potentials. The least reduction of such potency is thought; the fullest reduction will be to an act of its own.

Being, therefore, does no more than affirm of an object essence and existence, meaning and extramentality. However, meaning and extramentality can be related to each other in many ways. There is therefore no uniformity entailed in being. But a non-uniform denotation is not a form, which must be *una forma,* i.e., uniform. It is a quasi-form, a construct when used as a class for all and any beings; the expression of the intuition of reality when referred to different beings. If being is plural and multiple, then the famous "being-as-such" can only be a construct, for it is not referred univocally to its inferiors. But an ambiguous form is no form at all, because a form defines and confines.

Being-as-such is therefore a construct derived from the recognition that beings are plural and not homogeneously real. It is a legitimate construct because all reality involves an essence-existence relationship, and all beings have this relationship, not identically but equally. Being-as-such, therefore, is not a univocal, i.e., homogeneous, notion, but rather a non-homogeneous notion. However, it is not heterogeneous, because the relationship it represents is equal, even though not identical, but the equality is not of thing to thing, but of relationships to relationships. This is a proportional equality, and so, being is an analogous construct to permit the intuition of being to be predicated of every object capable of such an intuition.

However, we must avoid the confusion of the empiricist nominalist. He considers being as a shorthand symbol for the totality of a construct referred to an object. For him, therefore being can never be a predicate, an attribute, of an object. It says nothing beyond what was already said in the subject of a proposition. This was the burden of the observations made by Professor Stace in his controversy with Jacques Maritain at the Midcentury Convocation of Massachusetts Institute of Technology in 1949.[10] For Stace, to say that man is a being, is only a tautology, for it must be reduced to "man is a man," which by nominalist reduction says:

---

[9] *Sosein*: being such, i.e., essence. *Dasein*: being there, being in the world, i.e., existence.

[10] Cf. *Midcentury,* ed. by Burchard (New York: John Wiley and Sons, 1950).

"By man I mean man," which permits a logical reduction to: "the meaning of man is identical with the meaning of man."

The nominalist does not believe that things in themselves have meanings. Only words have meanings, and these are established by convention. In other words things do not have essences, i.e., intrinsic meanings. Being is a symbol for the totality of the existent, and therefore like the existent is meaningless. In such a supposition, being cannot be a predicate, for it gives no meaning to the subject other than that which the subject already carries with it.

Now in a realistic metaphysic *being* is an expression of the intuition of reality, and that intuition is meaningful. The "is" of the logical copula expresses either *Sosein* or *Dasein,* meaning or act, essence or existence. In fact, it always expresses both, but it may express one directly and the other indirectly, because "is" is meaningful only in terms of essence *and* existence. "Is" can be significant directly as existence, at least possible existence, and as such says more than mere meaning. It can therefore be an attribute, a predicate. However, "is" will not be a category, for, as act, it lies beyond or transcends the field of categories which are used as classes of meanings. But there is an intelligibility of being beyond categories because meaning is only one phase of reality. Meaning is contained in the intuition that meaning is extramental, but the extramentality of meaning is not contained in meaning as such. It is contained in the intuition of which meaning was one element.

Summary

(1) "Being" is the reduction of the verb "is" to the status of form.

(2) The verb "is" affirms the object of awareness to be intelligible and extramental, in the sense that the structure of the object is reflected by the mind and not created by it.

(3) This is made patent in existential judgments, e.g., John is tired, and in judgments of meaning or essence, e.g., a triangle is a plane figure formed by three sides.

(4) Essence and existence are the ultimate reductions of "is."

(5) Both are affirmed in "is," always, but one directly and the other indirectly.

(6) Therefore every being involves an essence and existence relationship.

(7) Though this relationship always involves the same terms, the relationship is not always the same.

(8) This can be seen in the essence of the infinite and the essence of the finite. In the infinite there is no confining effect due to essence, since essence is as big as the existence and is identical with it. In the finite

the essence contracts the area of actuality to a category of being. Essence and category go hand in hand. It is not without reason that the mystics call God the no-thing, i.e., the uncircumscribed act. The intelligibility of God lies in his act, which is his only essence.

This is again evident in accidents. Their act is that of the substance which they modify. They have no act of their own, except ideally. The book is red, and redness is an ideal object.

(9) Being therefore means different connotations in different contexts, but it is always equal, where equality means that discourse permutations of factors on different sides of the equation are possible.

(10) This equality is not the presence of the same form on both sides of the equation, but rather the presence of a quasi-form.

(11) This quasi-form is the essence-existence relationship involved in all being as attainable by the human intellect.

(12) Hence the equality is of relationships, and no identity, even logical, is implied.

(13) Because the equality is between relationships rather than things, the equality denying identity is called analogous, with the analogy of proportionality.

(14) The intuition of being in every instance is univocal with reference to the object intuited; it is analogous with reference to *different* objects.

(15) Being-as-such, the ultimate class or category, is no true class because of this analogy, and it is a construct of the mind. Being-as-such cannot exist, only this or that kind of being.

Excursus on obediential potency

The *Dynamis-Energeia* intuition of Aristotle led Saint Thomas to his Potency-Act doctrine. The historical investigations in the last fifty years have made it very clear that Thomas was much more than an expositor of Aristotle, even in the peculiarly original insights of the Stagirite. Thomas remade Aristotle wholly, so that even the basic notions in the Peripatetic philosophy took on a change.

Nor is it a true insight to say that Thomas was merely adjusting Aristotle to Catholic dogma. Thomas never made philosophy in this way. He did not believe in a "party-line" as the correct way of thinking. Thomas was a sincere believer. In terms of his faith, Christian dogma was an acquisition of truth, and in his reflective thought he took this truth into account, not in order to follow a "party-line" but in order to make all truth cohesive.

The Act-Potency of Aristotle did not go beyond his Matter-Form metaphysic. For Thomas this was too narrow a framework for truth as he had
experienced it. He broadened Act-Potency beyond the Matter-Form
framework, though he was stuck with Aristotelian language in the development of his doctrine. The ultimate potency for Thomas was not undefinable matter, but the Divine Idea. Thomas was not stuck with merely
empirical data; other data could also come into play in his philosophy
and speculations. In the enlargement of the Aristotelian framework,
Thomas was going back to Plato, but of this he was not fully aware,
though the suspicion was not altogether absent.

The Thomistic notion of "nature" is very different from the meaning
attached to it by the naturalist. For Thomas it was something metaphysical; an essence as the determinant of action. For Thomas physical did
not mean what it means today, something material. For Thomas it meant
something that existed and acted. When the present-day naturalist calls
an intelligent soul metaphysical, Thomas would have been nonplused.
The soul was for him just as physical as the body, although it was de-
cidedly spiritual. Even the metaphysical was not something unreal, but
wholly real with a reality that was ideal, and this ideal reality could be
actuated in the physical order, though not necessarily as a material substance.

A nature for Thomas was a metaphysical reality. It was verified in physical things by the physical substance, which was only a participation of
the metaphysical reality. Things in the physical order were not ultimate
natures, but participations of a nature, which was prior to and independent of the physical participants.

Any nature could with a slight modification do things which were
not ordinary to itself. In other words there were latent possibilities in a
nature which could not be called into play by the mere existence of the
nature in the existential world of participation. However, the Lord of
creation could produce the change in the nature. The latent possibilities
whose potency did not require actualization and which could not be
actualized by mere intercourse with physical agents of the finite order
were obediential potencies.

In this notion we have a valid expression of the act-potency theory.
The obediential potency must be in the agent. It is more than the possibility of something. It is truly a power in an agent, but a power which
will never be brought into play by the agent or by the stimulus of agents
that surround and condition his activity. Thus a horse has no obediential
potency to form concepts, because if he had, he would be in potency to
rationality, but that is excluded by the meaning of horse, which is a non-

rational agent. A thinking horse is nonsense. The minute the horse thinks, no matter what be the shape and figure of his body, he is a human being. In such an event there would be no actualization of an obediential potency but a transformation, a substantial change, made possible by the capacity of prime matter to be anything.

In the question of the intuition of God, or an act of supernatural faith preparing the way for the intuition, we leave man human but we heighten his capacities—obediential potencies. There is in man the power of seeing God, because man is intelligent and intelligence has as its highest action intuition. The intuition of God is thus within the absolute power of man, though it is not required that it be actualized either by the specific nature of man or by his natural surroundings.

3

The Epistemological Problem: Psychological Answers

We have seen the metaphysical answers to the question, how can the numinous be known?; now let us see some of the psychological answers. The difference between a psychological and a metaphysical answer lies in the fact that the metaphysical answer resolves the problem into the ultimate factors contained therein, while a psychological answer just indicates the genetic process involved in a phenomenon. The psychological answer sticks to the phenomenon and explains by correlating the phenomenal factors entailed.

Suggestion

The word "suggestion" is usually understood in a pejorative sense, though the word is innocent enough. Suggestion is the non-rational communication of an idea. Sheer tradition is always a suggestion-phenomenon.

Human nature is suggestionable. The little child acquires most of his ideas through suggestion and tradition. Suggestion is the beginning of intellectual life. When the child asks: what is that?, he wants a double answer and accepts both facets of the answer in the same way, by suggestion. He wants to know the name that society gives to the object of which the infant is aware, and he also wants to know the distinct nature of the phenomenon. In the beginning he is perfectly satisfied with suggestion, though with time he learns to suspect it.

In this primitive form of suggestion we have its nature depicted. Human beings are spontaneously suggestionable. It is the gateway to learning. Children are more suggestionable than adults. Women are more suggestionable than men, because women, being eminently existentialists and pragmatists, are not so enamored of theoretical grasps of objects. This latent indifference to pure theory inclines them to be suggestionable in such matters, though they will not be so suggestionable in the order of the practical. Unschooled men are more suggestionable than schooled products.

Primitive suggestionability soon becomes restricted by resistance to suggestion. This resistance is the effect of experience, which shows that suggestions can be and often are misleading. That is why the educated man is always more resistant to suggestion than the uneducated man. He has seen how suggestion has led men astray in history, and he has seen how it has led him astray. Excessive resistance to suggestion is unhealthy, and complete invulnerability to suggestion is impossible. Excessive resistance to suggestion is usually nothing but a defense mechanism in a human being who is highly suggestionable. This very fact makes him a ready prey to suggestions. He resists all suggestion on principle, and if the suggestion is given to him negatively, he will accept it readily. In adolescents the dare is an obvious example. It is suggested to the youth that he cannot do something, and his resistance to the suggestion makes him do the thing. If the thing had been asked for in its simplicity, he would not have done it at all.

Suggestion has been studied intensely. At the end of the last century it was the object of medical consideration, especially in the work of Dr. J. M. Charcot at La Salpetriere in Paris. The so-called Nancy School, under the impulse of Bernheim, continued this work and Dr. Coue some forty years ago wished to cure all kinds of ills by autosuggestion with his famous line: "Every day in every way I am getting better and better." Dr. Baudouin of the same school has continued the study without going to the extremes of Coue.

There are in general two forms of suggestion: heterosuggestion and autosuggestion. In autosuggestion the subject himself spontaneously or reflexly communicates to himself an idea non-rationally. In heterosuggestion the communication is made by someone other than the subject. Both forms of suggestion may be exercised simultaneously and in collaboration.

The basis of all advertisement is suggestion, and the psychology of advertisement is well known. The basic secret of successful suggestion is the overcoming of resistance. This can be done in many ways. The fundamental truth to be retained by the suggestioner is that resistance is a product of experience; man is naturally suggestionable. Hence it is important to provoke action that is spontaneous, where the reflective activity is nil or small. Another truth to be borne in mind is that man is subject to the law of fatigue. Resistance to suggestion, since it is not spontaneous, must be exercised with effort, and continued effort grows weaker. The third truth to be borne in mind is that the affective aura of an idea makes an idea attractive or repellent. Attractive ideas are readily accepted while repellent ideas are shunned. From these general truths we can draw concrete forms of suggestion.

Hypnosis

Ever since the days of Dr. Mesmer in the eighteenth century hypnotism has been seriously studied. The old "animal magnetism" proposed by Paracelsus (seventeenth century) and popularized by Mesmer has been rejected. Hypnotism is nothing but induced sleep. There are different levels of it giving rise to the distinction of light hypnosis and deep hypnosis. In deep hypnosis catalepsy—rigidity and automatism—can be produced, though this is rare. The normal state is somnambulism. This is no true trance, for the person hypnotized does not lose consciousness, which is evident by the possibility of understanding suggestions. However, the quality of awareness is very poor.

Deep hypnosis is produced by using light, by gentle strokes on the head or face, by monotonous sounds, by passes of the hand or movement of objects, by verbal suggestion. Methods have been devised and doctors study and use them. In the sleep state, no reflection is possible, and so the subject is prone to suggestion. He is not open to all suggestions, and will reject some. It is the common opinion today that the subject will not go against his own moral code, though he may go against the moral code of his group because he does not sincerely and wholeheartedly accept it. Deep hypnosis is unquestionably the best state for successful suggestion.

Light hypnosis is the comatose state which is neither full sleep nor full wakefulness. It can easily be induced. Thouless suggests a comfortable chair in a dark room with the gaze fixed on a single point of light, e.g., a candle behind a small screen perforated in one point. In this state of relaxation effort is difficult, and the habit of resistance to suggestion is not exercised. Salesmen use this hypnosis frequently. The prospect is well-dined and well-wined, and put into a comfortable chair in a cozy room, preferably at night. He is in a highly suggestionable mood, even though not in a full hypnotic state.

Heightening the affective attraction of the idea

This is used extensively in advertisement. A beautiful actress is pictured using or speaking in favor of *Songe de minuit,* already attractive by its name, and it is suggested that the use of this perfume will give the user the glamor of the actress. In point of fact, the actress may not use it at all—but the *association* of the actress with the perfume gives prestige to the article. All advertisement using the sex instinct tries to enhance the attraction of its article by such association.

Negatively this technique is used by affirming or insinuating that only the advertised article can prevent some undesired event: body-odor, halitosis, social failures, unhappy marriage, failure to get married, low esteem of the community. Toothpastes will insinuate that they will prevent caries, or when government prevents such lies, will assert that they aid in the prevention of caries, which is true of rinsing the mouth with water. Sometimes society will not tolerate an exaggeration of the goodness of an idea by instilling fear of its negation. We saw an advertising campaign which wished to sell video sets by threatening parents that a home without video will produce an inferiority complex in the children. This went a little too far in boldness and popular anger ended the campaign along these lines. Yet the fear element is strong in modern advertising. Unless you use soap X, you will be a social pariah. Unless you subscribe to magazine Y, you will be an ignoramus. Unless you have apparatus Z, you will not be able to hold your head up in the community.

Stressing and heightening the prestige of the suggestioner

In children suggestion is more powerful in proportion to the importance they give to the person who makes the suggestion. A parent can produce a mental assent with greater ease than others; an older person has more power than a child companion. This moving power can be called authority or prestige. It is presumed by human beings that certain individuals know more than others; however, more than mere knowledge is required in the suggestioner. He must be trusted, and trust always involves a love reaction. There are people who are outstanding for the wide range and accuracy of their knowledge, but their suggestions are neither welcome nor accepted. The gad-flies of society, like Socrates, fare badly in the hands of the community. Legend is usually substituted for fact in the popular mind, and the man who "debunks" the legend is not admired or loved. He is only hated, for the object of his suggestion is unpleasant. Some freer spirits will be moved but the community at large is repelled. The prestige of the suggestioner must be correlated to the affective attraction of the idea that he is trying to suggest.

The use of this principle in advertising is evident. Testimonials of recommendation by persons admired and trusted by the community carry weight. Youngsters who saw Hopalong Cassidy on the television screen trusted him. His recommendation of articles was a powerful suggestion on the children. The effect has been the incredible sale of countless articles of the Hopalong Cassidy label. The advertising agencies for the tobacco industry use persons of prestige in all walks of life to recommend their products, and they do so because this method of advertising sells a great many cigarettes.

Repetition of suggestion

Since it requires effort to resist suggestion and since this effort is limited by energy limits, pushing the suggestion beyond such limits will give the suggestion the opportunity it needs. Repetition is the simplest form of going beyond the limits of resistance.

In advertising this is well known. The advertiser looks for a simple slogan or jingle that is easily remembered and repeats it indefinitely. Cigarette people must keep up an expensive advertising program. If they stop, their sales go down.

It is most fascinating to see the number of jingles and slogans that we retain in memory and which we hear over and over again. "Schlitz, the beer that made Milwaukee famous"; "Coca-Cola, the pause that refreshes"; "Chesterfields, they satisfy." In some cases a mere name is dinned into our consciousness: Pepsodent, Ford, Arrow shirts, Jell-O, Borden. In a propitious situation we find ourselves asking for these products with no rational motive at all. The suggestion has worked. Sheer repetition has worn down resistance.

Suggestion and the assent to the numinous

That tradition and education, the media used by suggestion, influence religious beliefs is evident. Parental religion is easily transmitted to children, and we hear the facile but superficial statement: I belong to X Church because my people were X believers. There are family and national traditions which have tremendous suggestive power. This is seen by the geographic restrictions of famous religions. In a given culture where the members are homogeneous in their acceptance of that culture, religious visions are identical, and beyond the culture, the vision may be almost totally absent. Most religions have a vision that can only be transmitted by tradition. Catholicism, having its roots in a revelation to be recounted to others, leans very heavily on tradition, which is highly suggestive.

Religions also use peculiar media of suggestion. Some of the American Indian religious feasts employ narcotics to produce deep hypnosis. The Delphic Oracle threw the pythoness into a trance by exposing her to the gases of the Delphic cave. Temples are apt settings for light hypnosis. A darkened church, soft music, flickering candles, odor of incense, vastness of the structure, all contribute to a hypnotic state. In such an environment suggestion has great power. In prayer, that most distinctive manifestation of religion, certain postures and conditions are required. In some schools much stress is put on these things, and in yoga posture and position are given incredible importance. Most masters of prayer will recommend a quiet, darkened room and the hours of the night or early morning.

The attractive aura of the religious idea is heightened in many ways. Man is instinctively gregarious and the communal commitment is good. That is why scattered dissidents in a community eventually accept the religious scheme of the community. Isolated Catholics in a non-Catholic community become Baptists or Methodists, and vice-versa. If the first generation can still exercise its resistance, the second generation finds it difficult to do so.

Any kind of martyrdom is unpleasant and religious persecution, if maintained long enough, will practically eliminate a determined religion in a certain place. The believer is given three choices: suffering, conversion, or exile. Continued suffering will be chosen by only a very few. Conversion or exile will be the choices of the others, and the religion under persecution disappears. North Africa was totally Catholic until the arrival of Islam, but it is totally Mohammedan now, and only recent Christian missionary activity has made some little dent on this situation.

Religion always heightens the prestige of its spokesmen. The priest or parson is surrounded with an aura produced by segregation, peculiar garb, communal reverence and respect. The words of such men or women carry with them great suggestive power.

As for repetition, it is the stock in trade of all religions. How many times do we not see the cross, the symbol of Christianity, in a Christian culture. Catholicism lays great stress on material symbols which tend to become ubiquitous. Holy words are uttered over and over again, even in blasphemy, which latter all religions fight because it cheapens the word and robs it of its peculiar meaning, and suggestive force.

The limits of suggestion

To say that the religious idea is communicated by suggestion is hardly an admission that *only* suggestion produces religious assent. Suggestion is not all-powerful, not even in hypnotic states. Suggestions accepted in childhood universally disappear in adult people. The child has no difficulty in accepting the stork theory of birth, but a grown person cannot accept it, because it goes counter to his experience. Suggestion has a place in the initial appearance of religious assent, but it cannot assure the continuance of such an assent. Religions, with great powers of suggestion in their favor, have disappeared and nothing can bring them back. To most suggestions in favor of a given religion, there is a counter-suggestion exercised by a rival religion or irreligious vision of reality. Suggestion alone does not explain the survival of a religion either in an individual or in a community. The suggestion must be confirmed by experience and must make experience more luminous. As soon as experience begins to contradict a religious vision, that vision goes. Suggestion works as long as there is no criticism, but life brings to all men a critical spirit.

Communities which have a religious vision principally on the *ipse dixit* of a leader who uses his prestige tyrannically will in the future generations drop the vision. Anti-clericalism is the inevitable reaction to a clerical tendency to too much authority. The foreign pastor, who wielded so much power in the foreign-born parishes of this country, had to give way to a different kind of pastor. The new generation simply would not accept his *ipse dixit*. His humanity became too visible for him to be a god. Religious guides and teachers must be very careful not to insist too much on their authority and prestige, for as soon as it is questioned, it really is gone. This is especially true when dealing with adolescents who are entering into the critical stage of life. Prestige must be sought for these groups but in terms meaningful to them. The guide and teacher must manifest those qualities which are spontaneously esteemed by adolescents: kindness, understanding, and intellectual, artistic, and athletic prowess.

The validity of suggestion in religion

The tendency to consider suggestion as an invalid source of assent is widespread. There is some reason for this phenomenon, for suggestion can be used effectively for the communication of false ideas. However, it is not only the false that can be communicated by suggestion but also the true. Hence the use of suggestion is not of itself to be condemned; only the use of suggestion to communicate the false is to be deprecated.

It is impossible to avoid the use of suggestion where there is communication. A university teacher tries to communicate by presenting proof, and this is not of itself suggestion. However, it is inevitable that the professor likes an idea or dislikes it. He will present the arguments of a disliked idea in such a way as to deprive it of moving force and he will use all his power to communicate the ideas which he likes, and he will use suggestion, consciously or unconsciously. Every professor is at heart a missionary, and were he not, his teaching would be most unsuccessful. It is not usual for the man who knows the most or who is the most detached to be the sought-for professor. It is rather the teacher who can stimulate, satisfy, and engender enthusiasm who is the idol of the campus. This man is using suggestion all the time. The little ironic twist that he uses when he explains the position of those whom he dislikes, the gleam and glow that he gives to the exposition of the position that he likes, are all media of suggestion.

In religion it will not be different. The missionary zeal is a consequent of the divine encounter. If a revelation has been achieved the believer will communicate it and he will so communicate it that the listener is moved, by argument or without it. Much of a religious vision must be communicated by suggestion, because most people have neither the time nor the inclination to analyze the doctrine rationally.

The tactic of the Communists in this question is very illuminating. They accuse religion of being an idea communicated exclusively by suggestion. They do everything possible to undo this suggestion. They deliberately inaugurate campaigns of vilification to rob the religious leaders of prestige. They use every means to prevent the religionists from reaching the public. They will suppress their schools and silence their organs of publicity. They will forbid any manifestation of the religious. They will prevent youth from having contacts with religious persons, and forbid these to mention religion to young people. They will present religious ideas with ridicule and mockery. They will penalize religious profession so as to make it unpleasant.

Yet what do they then do? They glorify their leaders to give them a prestige out of all reasonable proportion with the facts. They use journals, cinema, stage, and radio to sell their message. They monopolize education of youth and impose a program of indoctrination. None but orthodox, party-line Communists will be allowed to use these media of expression. Serene debate is not tolerated; orthodoxy alone has the floor. We have here high-pressure suggestion—and this from the critics of religion because it uses suggestion. In terms of calm rational discussion communism can never become the world-view of a people. There is needed heat, confusion, pressure, and suggestion. And the worst of it is, this uncomfortable atmosphere must be maintained, or the communist vision of the community disappears. The history of communist success has been a most unkind critic of communist ideas.

However, even though there is nothing illicit in the use of suggestion in the communication of religious ideas, even though it be inevitable that this means of communication be used, yet religionists must be warned against too great a faith in this medium. Just because suggestion communicates its ideas with no concern for reason, it makes the communication unstable. If it alone is employed, the religious ideas will die. There must go hand in hand with suggestion a rational presentation of the ideas, for only in this way will the suggested idea be able to survive.

Emotion

By "emotion" we mean what is also indicated by the word "feeling." It is the pleasure or pain content of an idea or an experience. Such content is difficult to express in concepts, because it is known as felt in experience without precise image. Such content is the concomitant of the experience of objects which are the center of attention and capable of accurate conceptual expression. The concomitant feeling-tone of the experience is a peripheral object of awareness, vivid enough but not clear and distinct. Yet the emotions are so important in life because man flees from pain in any form and hurries toward pleasure. Such pursuit and flight is the ultimate explanation of all human action.

Intellection in itself is free from such pursuit, for it looks for truth. However, intellection is not isolated. It is an action of a pleasure-seeking agent, subject to will-thrusts and influenced by will pursuits. Can the emotions induce an assent to the numinous?

Before we can answer this question, we must define two important terms: reason and rationalization. When an assent is reasoned, the assent follows on an analysis of the meaning of the assent in the light of the principles of thought. If the meaning of the assent is dictated by the principles of thought, the assent is reasoned. Thought is, however, operative on levels higher than logic, and a reasoned assent may prescind from logic, though it can never contradict it. Intellectualism is not identical with rationalism.

An assent can also be made under the dictamen of the will just because the assent is pleasurable. The intellect can then reflect on the assent and show rational argument for it, but these arguments are made after the assent has been made and they had no part in the forming of the actual assent. The subsequent argumentation is called rationalization. This process has been known in all the history of mankind. The sophists, as described by Socrates in Plato, made rationalization the only form of intellection, because they were totally indifferent to the answer in truth, and would give reasons for both sides of a question. Implicitly they held that man could not reach the objective truth, and that argumentation was only a kind of a game played to achieve legal or forensic justification of actions and stands. The sophists were interested in making debaters and lawyers, not philosophers, i.e., lovers of the truth. They were skeptical and the skepticism led to cynicism.

Now we tackle our question: does emotion engender the assent to the numinous? We shall analyze certain kinds of emotions.

Nature emotions

It is hardly a great discovery to say that a man is emotionally influenced by the natural framework of his activity. A dark, sultry day produces sadness or listlessness in human beings. Excessive cold prevents activity just as much as excessive heat. An agreeable temperature must be achieved to make life pleasant, and the mere achievement of this temperature may take up all of man's energy. The creative impulses and the pushes toward discovery can have no play, and man in these circumstances is not happy, though he may be resigned.

However, nature can offer man a panorama that fills him with gladness. There is a soothing vastness in the sea seen from a grassy shore. There is awe engendered by high peaks, solemn and silent in somber colors, looming over an observer. The emotional stimulus in nature has affected all peoples and all cultures. For a romantic such stimulus can be very great. The sea poetry of the English and the mountain poetry of the Germans clearly prove this. Even the humanist is not immune to the influence of Nature, although he looks for different phases of it. The

44   PSYCHOLOGICAL ANSWERS

Roman writers were afraid of the sea and the high mountains, as is clear
in Livy, Virgil, and Horace; however, they loved the brooks, the hills,
the groves, and the fertile country-side.

The religious sentiment, the feeling constellation that accompanies
the achievement of the numinous, is the complex of awe, fear, love, and
trust. Something like this can be excited by Nature. William James
quotes a passage of Thoreau.

> Once, a few weeks after I came to the woods, for an hour I doubted whether
> the near neighborhood of man was not essential to a serene and healthy
> life. To be alone was somewhat unpleasant. But, in the midst of a gentle
> rain, while these thoughts prevailed, I was suddenly sensible of such sweet
> and beneficent society in Nature, in the very pattering of the drops, and in
> every sight and sound around my house, an infinite and unaccountable
> friendliness all at once, like an atmosphere, sustaining me, as made the
> fancied advantages of human neighborhood insignificant, and I have never
> thought of them since. Every little pine-needle expanded and swelled with
> sympathy and befriended me. I was so distinctly made aware of the presence
> of something kindred to me, that I thought no place could ever be strange
> to me again.[1]

Ideas produce emotions, but emotions can produce ideas. This is clear
enough in adolescents who without previous briefing come to some confused knowledge of erotic action. There is something instinctive here,
undoubtedly, but the idea is as much the product of emotion as it is of
the mere instinct.

The vastness of Nature, her power and mysteriousness, her capacity
for producing pleasant feeling, can easily lead to something that we
can call a natural mysticism; all persons remember some vivid experiences along this line. An easy rationalization of the experience is to
personify Nature. The result would be the concept of the numinous.

The primitives certainly fell into this temptation. They saw personality
in so many aspects of nature: dryads, fauns, nymphs, genii, and so forth.
What is more, they gave to such personifications religious worship, though
in all probability they did not consider these beings as truly numinous,
but rather earth-spirits.

Religions, even though they are far removed from Nature-worship,
still use Nature-symbols in their approach to the numinous. In Catholic

---

[1] William James, *The Varieties of Religious Experience* (New York: Longmans,
Green & Co., 1907), p. 275. Quoted by permission of the publishers. This is an abridged
version from the Riverside edition of *Walden*, p. 206, published by The Houghton
Mifflin Company, who have also given permission.

worship Christ is the Sun of Justice, Mary is the Star of the Sea and the Mystical Rose. In the Scriptures Yahweh thunders on Sinai.

Religious men and women recognized the relationship of similarity between nature-emotions and religious emotions. Ignatius of Loyola employs this similarity in order to pass from the natural to the numinous plane. In the First Week of the Exercises which strives for sorrow and shame because of sin, the instructions are to meditate in a darkened room, to abstain from joyful liturgy, to use ascetical practices of fasting and penance. On the contrary, when in the Fourth Week he seeks for joy and gladness, he instructs the retreatant to seek the sunshine and the flowers, to take part in the liturgy.

However, Nature is not beneficent in all her aspects. She can be quite repellent. This fact helps to explain the dualism of Zoroasterian religion and its Christian modification, Manicheism. Nature in her two aspects suggested two deities; one good and the other bad. Did the African scene influence Saint Augustine in his adoption of Manicheism and did it stick with him in part even in his Catholic days? Such was the accusation of Julian of Eclanum in the days of Augustine himself.

There is much nature-emotion in Saint Francis of Assisi, and his religion was quite optimistic, even though he knew nature both as kind and unkind. Sister Sun, Sister Moon, were joined by Brother Wolf, who certainly was not a kindly apparition. Even the fire which was preparing the cauterizing iron was addressed in the usual way: Sister Fire, be kind. The answer, of course, is that Saint Francis did not get his numinous experience from Nature, but rather he explained Nature in the light of the numinous, acquired another way.

Conclusions

(1) Nature can arouse a sentiment like that proper to the numinous.

(2) It is easy to personify Nature in the warmth of the emotion.

(3) The similarity of the emotion does not mean identity of the object exciting the emotion with the numinous object.

(4) Because there is a difference, Nature does not carry with it the notion of the totally other, and Nature-religion readily assumes a pantheistic form.

(5) Not all aspects of Nature are propitious for an emotion like that aroused by the numinous because Nature has an unpleasant side.

(6) The numinous, already achieved, can explain Nature with a greater ease than Nature can emotionally engender a God-concept.

(7) Nature can be used by religious persons in their pursuit of the

numinous as a pragmatic means, with no confusion in their minds
that Nature is the numinous.

(8) For Saint Paul (*Romans* 1, 19-20) Nature leads to God by way of
reasoning. The finite and contingent character of Nature by the
logic of relationships points to the existence of God. In such a use
of Nature, there is no rationalization but rather true reasoning.

Moral emotions

Except for extreme psychopathic cases, no human being seems to be
amoral, though different codes of morality are used by different men.
Man evidently is committed to morality by being human.

Yet this universal acceptance of moral norms as true obligations does
not bring with it the moral excellence portrayed by the different moral
codes. Saint Paul described well the moral conflict that is at the core of
human consciousness (*Romans* 7, 14-25).

The impulse toward moral action has been described in all literatures
as law, and this very name indicates how easy it is to rationalize the
moral emotion, the feelings aroused by the moral impulse, by postulating
a law-maker. Conscience is called by the poets the voice of God. It isn't.
It is my voice. Kant saw this clearly, but even he recognized that conscience postulated the existence of God. Only through conscience and
the emotional thrust behind it would he admit that God's existence could
be proved, where the proof is not a syllogism demonstrating his existence
but an analysis of moral emotion to show that it postulates God's existence.

Even Sigmund Freud could not overcome this line of thought. He
admitted no numinous reality but explained it as a projection of the
Oedipus complex, which also created the feeling of moral obligation.

All religions connected morality with the numinous. The gods were
vindicators of the moral code and they punished violators and rewarded
observers. Tabu, no matter what may have been its original function
and meaning, in development was always related to the numinous.

However, the religiosity produced by moral emotions is a very dry
religion. Calvinism in all its forms, especially in American Puritanism,
was a moralistic religion. The Calvinists were enamored of Christian simplicity as manifested in the primitive Christians and this they tried to imi-
tate. The result was that their religious meeting houses were robbed of all
decoration and left bare and plain. For liturgy a moralistic sermon of
great length and seriousness was substituted. Psalms were indeed sung, but

many churches refused to permit an organ or other form of accompaniment, as being inconsistent with the moral simplicity of Christianity.

In Kant, religion was reduced to moralism, for he denied the possibility of meeting God either by reason or by revelation. This tendency, so pronounced in Kant, is proper to all who approach divinity through morality. It is not an exaggeration to say that they invent religion as an aid to morality, rather than make morality a phase of religion. To a positivistic minded thinker this kind of religiosity can be attractive, and therefore we shall find it prominent in the minds of men who are skeptical of intellection, especially when it becomes highly metaphysical. It explains in part the spirit of tolerance of different religions in this country. In most Christian religions the code of morality is substantially the same, and therefore to a man with a moralistic preoccupation in religion, these religions are all equally valid. For these men holiness is identified with moral perfection; and it has no other meaning, much less the real meaning, union with God.

The intellectualism so deep in Catholicism does not permit such moralism to become predominant. The end of religion is to unite man to God through an intellectual sharing of the divine being. This purpose is completely amoral, and morality has no part in this final fruit of religion. This does not mean that Catholicism is indifferent to morality; it insists that moral rectitude is a prerequisite but not the cause of this union. The Sacraments, causes of the union, are more stressed than the moral law.

Yet in Catholicism we find movements that were moralistic. The Fathers of the Desert and the first Monks of the West were interested in flying from sin. Moral failure was their great fear and to overcome it they fled from the world where they believed moral perfection was impossible. The Fathers of the Desert relinquished many of the essential features of Catholicism. They took no part in the liturgy and in the beginning they avoided social contacts, though before very long they did form loosely-united communities under an abbot. The monks did pray, the psalms for example, but the value for them was as much ascetical exercise as the lifting of the heart to God. The great text of Scripture for them was the one referring to the taking of the Kingdom of Heaven by violence.

Jansenism was a recrudescence of moralism. The nuns of Port Royale would not go to communion because they were not morally prepared for it, though their moral conduct was not only exemplary but very severe. The Jansenists were undoubtedly influenced by Calvinism but did not reach its extremes because they deduced their vision of life from the writings of Saint Augustine, who, though demanding a high morality, was pessimistic of realizing it without a union with God expressing itself in love.

In the Augustinian approach we have another way in which moral emotion can lead to God. Moral failure is the experience of all men. This causes deep distress. When repeated attempts are made to achieve moral perfection but all attempts are futile, man looks elsewhere for aid. The numinous who can cancel out past failure and produce future success is an easy construct for a man in this position. This was the essence of Luther's conception of Christianity. He found that monastic asceticism, which he practised as faithfully as he could, did not bring him the moral perfection proper to a Christian. His readings of Saint Augustine and of Saint Paul suggested to him the solution. A vital adhesion to God by emotion would rid him of past failures and assure him of future success. This was not the answer of Saint Augustine. He came to a vivid realization of the core of the Christian message, namely that God alone can assure moral excellence in a man, and man must therefore throw himself on God by complete incorporation into the Church, through the media of faith, sacraments, and love.

The Catholic doctrine on sin has two features which are psychologically sound. First of all, the insistence that morality is only possible by God's grace and that God, being good, will give this grace to those who seek for it. This avoids what Thouless calls the *Law of Reversed Effort*.[2] Preoccupation with an evil can bring about the evil feared. If a six-inch board is placed on the floor anyone can walk it. However, if that board be placed between two forty-story buildings, the situation is different. Fear will suggest falling and the probability is very high that the individual, unless trained in this sort of thing, will fall. Sheer negation is impossible. If we are told not to think of an elephant for thirty seconds, we shall think of the elephant, for the negation is meaningful only in terms of the affirmation. The elephant will then have a suggestive power. Concentration on sin will psychologically produce sin. If, however, we are told that God will take care of us, the dangerous preoccupation will disappear. With the preoccupation gone, trials will be met fearlessly and triumphantly. For religious guides this principle is very important. Most individuals have moral problems of one kind or another. It is the work of the guide to rid the individual of fear which must be replaced by a force more positive. Protestantism uses this very much in the conversion

---

[2] Robert H. Thouless, *An Introduction to the Psychology of Religion* (Cambridge University Press, 1923), p. 52.

phenomenon, but as used it does not seem to be very efficacious. "Backsliding" is a well-known reaction to conversion and the "hitting-of-the-sawdust-trail." The whole technique of the revival is emotional suggestion with little rational basis to the whole thing. The love of God is not possible without a knowledge of God. Ignatius of Loyola put it well in his approach to conversion—to know God better in order to love him more with a view to imitating him more closely. That is the true road to conversion.

The second feature in Catholicism which takes care of moral emotions is the institution of confession. It is not true to say that Catholic confession is a predecessor of the Freudian analysis. There is all the difference in the world between the two things. The Freudian does not believe in objective guilt, because he believes neither in liberty of the will nor in an objective moral code. It is true that the Freudian achieves much good in the mere catharsis of confession, but this is not why he uses the confession. He is not even interested in the confession for itself, because he wishes to get behind the things confessed in order to discover the unconscious root of the difficulty. Catholic confession does not wish to get behind the confession, which is final in its order. The confession only shows whether or not the individual is in will estranged from God by an abiding disposition. If the confessor finds that he is not, the absolution or cancelling out of failure is given. Confession in its sacramental form, i.e., with absolution, rids the individual of the distressing emotion of past failure. He can begin again with the slate cleaned. Psychologically there is nothing better than such an institution and sects that had opposed confession have brought it back.

However, the whole value of confession consists in removing the past. It can nevertheless do just the contrary. If the penitent is so worried about the confession itself, it will be another element of distress. The integrity required by Catholic dogma must not be exaggerated into another pitfall for the penitent. A wise confessor will know how to put his penitent at ease in this matter. In the confessional his suggestive power is very high and he must use it to the advantage of the penitent.

Conclusions

(1) The moral emotions by a spontaneous rationalization of the "voice of conscience" as the expression of the will of a transcendental law-giver will easily lead to the God-concept.

(2) The emotions of moral failure, guilt-consciousness, can easily lead a man to the religious assent.

(3) All religions, even those which have no fixed morality of their own,

relate the numinous to morality, thus giving moral emotions a strong power in leading man to the religious.

(4) Moral emotions will not keep a man in religion, if the God-concept is not justified on rational grounds.

(5) Therefore moral emotions will not by themselves guarantee an abiding religious allegiance.

(6) Strict reasoning on the fact of moral emotions can validate an objective rational assent to the numinous. In such a case there is no rationalization of emotion but a true ratiocination.

Religious emotions

As we have seen, there is a religious sentiment, a peculiar constellation of emotions proper to religion. This sentiment is pleasant and this pleasurable element will secure religion against the attacks of atheists. These latter reduce religious satisfaction to the order of narcotic bliss, but even in this reduction they have made it clear that they will not get rid of religion any more than narcotic laws will stop narcoticism.

The God-encounter in religion, especially in its high point, prayer, is a highly exhilarating experience. Strange as it may seem, all men want to pray. Even atheists have invented prayer techniques to give men the prayer experience without a God-commitment. Prayer is not too common only because men do not know how to pray, and the different techniques are often either very boring or quite fruitless. Prayer is the God-encounter with all the religious emotions called into action.

Communal worship

Subjective cult. Cult is always a public act because it supposes a group in action, and in a group some external muscular action must take place. A subjective cult wishes to communicate to the participants the God-experience. Its prime aim is not the activity of the group directed toward the numinous already achieved by them, but rather the passivity of the group in order to make them ready for the felt action of God. There is no true sacramentalism in this form of worship, because the essence of the sacrament is that in a symbolic action the numinous is active without any consciousness of the individuals positing the act. In subjective cult God is experienced directly without medium, and the common meeting is only an occasion apt for such an experience. In all such cult the participants are conditioned for the experience. The community does not so much address itself to God, but rather prepares itself for God's address. All actions work on the participants, rather than the participants acting toward God.

The lowest form of this cult is the *orgiastic*. The intoxicating dances of the primitives, the frenzy of the Dionysiac and Orphic mysteries, the exuberance of the American frontier revivals, the exotic actions of the Holy Rollers and Pentecostals, all are examples of orgiastic cult. Their purpose is to induce the coming of the numinous in intense emotional encounter. The old phrase put it well: give me that old-time religion. The weakness of this kind of cult is that it is completely divorced from reason, which has no play whatever in the experience. This lack of objective control lays the whole experience open to trenchant criticism, for the role of suggestion is very high. The passing of the experience leaves little solid in the participant and onlookers at the cult are usually dismayed and disgusted by the uncontrollable emotionalism of it all.

A higher form is the theory of the *meeting of the Friends or Quakers*. They meet in calm sobriety and wait for "the coming of the Spirit." He who has the Spirit speaks in the Spirit. If the Spirit does not come, the meeting ends. In Quaker meetings there is no need of priest or preacher —though in modern times they do use preachers.

The highest form is the *Sermon meeting*. This is predominantly Protestant worship. Jewish worship, since the end of the Temple service, has been reduced to this. Catholic forms of it can be seen in retreats. In all these forms the participants are passive. The preacher does the work, though usually an emotional setting is produced by songs and music, and a suggestive background of beautiful architecture is used—though some Protestant sects are opposed to such helps.

In Protestant and Jewish theory, the preacher is not a real preacher, but rather a teacher and scholar. He explains the Book which is the source of achievement of the numinous. The Jewish rabbi is nothing sacerdotal. He is not even the leader of the community in theory. He is a scholar who knows the book well. But, the modern rabbi is not different in function from the Protestant minister. The latter, too, is an expositor of the Word, which he has studied. He arouses the listeners to depths of the Word which might have escaped them. The Word operates on the listeners and through the Word the numinous is achieved in the prayer experience. As Paul Tillich has said, Protestantism in its higher forms is a most intellectualistic religion.

However, its very intellectualism is its danger. The majority of people find no attraction in it. The result is that the preachers readily fall into the temptation of being orators striving for emotional effect. When they avoid this danger, they become moralistic. The sterility of the sermon meeting has been recognized by the Protestants who today have turned to liturgy which is a sacramental or objective form of cult.

In the subjective cult, it is not the community that speaks to God, but rather an occasion of God speaking to the individual members of the community. The meeting is used as a means for experience and is not truly the people of God in action. The weakness of such cult is seen by chaplains in the war areas. The Protestant chaplain has nothing that he can do for the soldiers. He does not possess the power of holy action. He can console and stimulate but he can do no more. The result is that the wounded soldier who is in no condition for words receives nothing from his religious guide and there seems no reason why he should be there at all.

However, let us make an observation that is necessary. The distinction between subjective and objective cult derives from James Bissett Pratt in his *The Religious Consciousness*.[3] This distinction is very illuminating and in substance sound. However, it will never be verified purely in any cult. Protestant and Jewish cult certainly expect God to work on the individual in the congregation rather than the congregation on God. Yet there are sacramental elements in Protestant and Jewish cult. The Protestant does retain the Lord's Supper and Baptism. These are symbols whereby the community approaches God and the community is sacerdotal in as far as its action is a holy one. However, this element must be subordinate in Protestant worship. In Catholic or Orthodox Byzantine worship the action is always primarily sacramental and sacerdotal, but there is a secondary purpose in the liturgy, namely, to teach the people and to arouse in them sentiments proper to the religious vision of the distinctive group. No cult is purely objective or subjective. One can only say that a cult is in tendency subjective or objective.

Objective cult. In an objective cult the purpose of the meeting is not the preparation of the participant for a God-visit, but rather the activity of the participant on the God-level. The participant does not go primarily to have his faith renewed but rather to exercise his faith with activities which suppose it. The action of the cult is not on the individual but is rather the action of the individual on the God-level. One speaks and acts with God. The media will be sacramental, i.e., symbols established by God whereby the community marches toward God.

In Roman Catholicism, High Anglicanism, and Byzantine Orthodoxy the supreme act of cult is the Mass or Liturgy. The people through the instrumentality of the priests offer to God the sacrifice of Christ. Com-

[3] New York: The Macmillan Co., 1937, chapter 14, p. 290 ff.

munion is also achieved through the symbol of the consecrated elements, but the cult is performed even by those who do not receive communion. Something is being done. A holy action is being posited by the people of God, who gave them the power to do so. There is divine power at work which the community recognizes by the faith it has. This faith is not produced by the action, but is rather the prior condition of it.

In subjective cult the use of a dead or peculiar language not possessed by the people at large would be contrary to the aim of the cult. Therefore the vernacular is of the essence of subjective cult. In **objective** cult it makes no difference what language is being used, or even **if no language is used**. The cult is essentially action. The Catholic's answer that he prays in Latin because God understands it perfectly is more than a witticism. The Protestant minister in his prayers, benedictions, and invocations usually talks to the community rather than to God. His rhetorical formula is God-directed, but his actual words are for the benefit of the people and contain reproaches, consolations, and exhortations to them. The prayers in the Mass are directed only toward God. They contain no address to the people.

It is the experience of objective cults that they soon take on language forms that are alien to the language of the community. Even the Protestant service will speak in Bible English or German, which is far removed from current English. This was clearly brought out by Ronald Knox in *Trials of a Translator*.[4] Coptic priests because of a meager education do not know how to translate the liturgy which they use, for Copt as used in the Mass is a dead language. The Slavonic used in the Slav Byzantine rites is not the living Slav but rather Church Slavonic, a dead language. There is nothing in Byzantine canon law forbidding the liturgy from being celebrated in a modern language and at times a modern language is used, but the people spontaneously use a hieratic language after a time. It is the otherness of the numinous that requires another mode of expression when action takes place on the numinous plane. The numinous must be veiled, and the curtains which were used about the altar in early times developed into the ikonastasis of the Byzantine churches.

Now it is true that a completely unknown tongue would easily pervert the cult into a meaningless jumble, but if the ministers and people know what they are saying and doing at least in a general way, the use of a foreign language, instead of being a hindrance, is really an asset.

It is to the credit of the Liturgical Movement that it wished to stress the active role of the participants in the liturgy. They were not to be passive spectators of an action but rather active partakers. Therefore to

---

[4] New York and London: Sheed and Ward, 1950.

pray the rosary while mass was going on was to be deprecated. The supporters of the Liturgical Movement urged a study of ecclesiastical Latin so that the participation of the faithful would be more intelligent, and some of the movement wish at least parts of the mass to be said in the vernacular, not so that the people understand what is going on, but so that they understand what they are doing.

Sacramentalism has the great advantage of being a cult where the people do something holy, directed to God who gave the people the power to do the holy thing, pleasing to God in the first place and useful for the people in the second place. When Protestants complain of the magical elements in Catholicism, they do put their finger on something essential to the cult, namely that actions are performed with power exercised beyond the natural capacity of the actions. However, this is not some secret natural force, or even a demonic energy, but a divine elevation of a material reality to the divine level. God is working in the work of the congregation. Paul Tillich along with other Protestants are scandalized with this pretension because they do not admit that God can in any way be materialized. As a result, these thinkers cannot admit of anything like a true incarnation of God. Yet even they cannot keep to the high plane which they set up for themselves. After all, G-O-D is a material symbol for God and the divinity is somehow contained in that symbol. If a dead word is a God-containing symbol, why cannot a pragmatic word, an action, be a God-containing symbol?

Although the objective cult uses symbols, it is clear that the subjective element of the cult is not excluded. The symbols are meaningful and as such they speak to the participants giving instruction, consolation, and exhortation. As we have said, no cult is merely objective or merely subjective.

Individual prayer

The religious man prays not only in groups but also alone. To achieve this kind of prayer, different forms are at his disposal.

Vocal prayer. In vocal prayer verbal formulae are recited by the individual. The formula itself is not prayer. It must elevate the individual to an experience of the numinous. As a rule, vocal prayer cannot produce a great and intense experience of the numinous, though it may be an initial step. Because of the difficulties of mental prayer most people stick to vocal prayer. For this purpose they use memorized formulae like the Pater Noster or have recourse to manuals of prayer. Even though the grasp on the numinous is not tight in this form of prayer, a general atmosphere of reverence for the mysterious numinous is produced and a vague awareness of God is achieved. This is equally true for mere attendance at religious cult or even a worshipful visit to a sanctuary.

Mental prayer. Saint Teresa of Avila describes the kind of prayer she found useful in the days of relaxed religious life. She would take a book, let us say the Scriptures or the Imitation of Christ by Kempis, read a passage, and then reflect on it. This reflection was an elevation of the heart and mind to God. As she found herself being drawn to other kinds of thinking, she would return to the book and read another passage.

Saint Ignatius used the same technique without a book. Instead of a printed passage he used a vocal prayer formula, and stopped the recitation to allow a reflection on its meaning in terms of the numinous. This he calls the Second Method of Prayer. He has also a Third Method, which consists of praying slowly so that the thoughts come spontaneously but not with great clarity or precision. He uses the breath as a measure of speed. One word is to be pronounced with every exhalation. There is here no connection with the breathing technique of yoga, where right breathing is required to exercise inner powers of man. In Ignatius it is only a slowing-up process to make possible a direction of the mind toward God under the influence of a word.

Discursive prayer is the use of the intelligence to raise man to the God awareness according to the general modes of intellection. The systematizer of this kind of prayer who had great influence on the prayer activity of Catholicism was Ignatius of Loyola. He proposed three forms of discursive prayer to which he gave the names of Meditation, Contemplation, and Application of the Senses.

Meditation, as defined in the little book, *Spiritual Exercises,* was the consideration of a theme, abstract in nature but specifically religious in terms of memory, understanding, and will. The functions of the will were to arouse the emotions proper to the theme and also to dictate proposals of action for the future.

Contemplation for Ignatius, though not for other masters of prayer, was the use of the memory, imagination, and will on some concrete story. In imagination the praying person would be present at the scene of the story and should hear and see what the people were saying and doing. He should make apt reflections, allow his will to evoke the corresponding emotions, and make the resolutions for future life in accord with the truths perceived.

Application of the Senses in the Ignatian sense means only an imaginative participation in an historical event of religious significance. It differs from a contemplation only in as far as no reflections are made and no formal resolutions posited.

In the Ignatian discursive prayer there is always room made for what Loyola calls the colloquy. This is the real prayer, when the mind leaves the theme of consideration to direct itself to God alone. Ignatius calls this conversation, colloquium, but he does not demand that words be used. They may be, but it is not of the essence. What is required is a confrontation of the soul with God as a loved object, personal and living.

It will be seen that Ignatian prayer is intellectual debate and imaginative reconstruction. What is more, these efforts are inducive of the colloquy where prayer is to be found in its purity. The discourse or imagery only lead to the colloquy concerning which Ignatius gives no formula except to say that we should converse with God as a friend, which of course is not telling us how this is to be done.

The weakness of the Ignatian technique is that it requires reasoning facility or image facility. Persons weak in these two kinds of activity find the Ignatian prayer method unfruitful. This was the verdict of Saint Teresa of Avila who made the exercises under Saint Francis Borja but did not find them helpful to her.

An older form of discursive prayer used both by Christians and non-Christians is the chaplet or Rosary. This form of prayer existed before Christianity and in Christianity it predated Saint Dominic. In fact, just what was Saint Dominic's part in the establishment of the Dominican Rosary is obscure. This is certain; the Rosary known today could not have existed before the sixteenth century, for the Ave Maria formula that we know seems to have had its origins in Mainz in the sixteenth century. Besides, there are other chaplets in Christianity in addition to the Dominican chaplet called Rosary.

In Buddhism, all monks have the Rosary or chaplet. It is one of the three things that a Buddhist monk may own. With Buddhists and Christians the technique is the same, but clearest in the Dominican Rosary. A string or chain contains 59 or 169 counters, which in the current Dominican Rosary are beads, though knotted Rosaries are not unknown. As the fingers run over the counters, an Ave Maria is said at each counter and on the counters that divide each group of ten a Pater Noster is said, and each group of ten is ended with a Gloria Patri. Now it is not the aim of the user to employ vocal prayer. The Paters and Aves are only a measuring device of time, and an occupation of the external senses. The prayer consists in a discursive consideration of a theme in the life of our Lord and our Lady.

The discursive thought need not be as concentrated as in Ignatian prayer. It is sufficient to train the attention of the mind to the "mystery" or historical incident under consideration. Since the time allotted to each "mystery" is short, the space of ten Aves, there is no danger of fatigue of attention.

In the Buddhist chaplet, no prayer is said on the counters. Instead the mystic formula "Om padhi aum" is said. The phrase is not the prayer, but rather a preparation for contemplation of the numinous.

The success of the Rosary in both Christianity and Oriental prayer-life is evident. Catholics almost without exception know this prayer form and use it sometimes; some use it often. It is the only form of discursive prayer with wide employment, though not a few "say" the Rosary with no attempt at meditation on the Mysteries.

In Teresan doctrine there is a higher form of mental prayer than the discursive. Saint Teresa calls it the prayer of Simplicity, though in other writers it is called the prayer of Simple Regard, or the prayer of the Presence of God. Saint Teresa makes it clear that this is a "natural" prayer, i.e., it requires no elevation of the faculties involved, and it can be acquired by practice. It is natural mysticism.

This prayer consists in directing the attention of the mind toward the living, all-pervasive God. No line of thought or debate is adopted and no resolutions of the will are made. The God-concept alone carries the mental action of the meditant. Formal concepts are not developed nor are they in place. The God-concept alone is maintained and a state of monoideism is induced. The effects are those of personal encounter, though the numinous is present only by reason of the concept with which the prayer began.

Saint Teresa and other spiritual writers hold this kind of prayer highly and consider it superior to all forms except supernatural mystical experience. That the prayer can be highly satisfying leaves no doubt. That it is easy to wander or lapse into day-dreaming is also evident. Most religious people for short periods, from time to time, do use this kind of prayer, and it probably is the colloquy of the Ignatian Meditations.

Mystical prayer. Of this kind of prayer, we shall speak later when dealing *ex professo* with the mystical phenomenon.[5]

The emotional effect of prayer, social or individual, is great. The consequences of revival meetings, retreats, Eucharistic congresses are incredi-

---

[5] Cf. A. Poulain, S.J., *Les Graces d'oraison* (Paris: Retaux, 1906). English title: *Graces of Interior Prayer,* trans. from the 6th ed. by L. L. Yorke Smith (St. Louis: Herder, n. d.).

ble. The man who desires conversion but cannot make the final step is invariably exhorted to pray. It is in prayer that he will come to his real assent to the numinous.

However, though the prayer emotions are very influential, we must animadvert that they do not validate the reality of the numinous. The prayer phenomenon is certainly a suggestion phenomenon, though it is a case of auto-suggestion. As we have seen, suggestion neither validates nor invalidates the object communicated.

Let us make a final observation. The prayer emotion must not be confused with the liturgical esthete. Liturgy is a symbolic pageant and as such it has the beauty of pageant and the attraction of art. There are those who derive keen satisfaction from solemn cult, performed with dignity and taste, in surroundings of beauty. It is not the numinous that interests the liturgical esthete but the beauty of the pageant. This beauty is of this world. Hunger for it is universal, and anti-religious groups adopt symbolic or liturgical pageants. Groups that are vaguely religious but adverse to any theological commitments, like the Masons, make much of liturgy in their own circles. However, this need not be and usually is not a prayer emotion.

The danger of prayer emotion is that it can descend to sheer emotionalism. When this is the situation, there is no contact with the numinous at all, or so little that it is not important.

The Influence of the Instincts

For the sake of convenience we shall adopt the classification of W. H. R. Rivers.[6] By "instinct" we mean a psychic preformation innate in a living subject whereby without previous education a set behavior pattern or act thereof, uniform in the species, results invariably from exposure to an apt stimulus. The instincts fall under three groups: self-conservation, race-conservation, and gregariousness.

Self-conservation impels us not merely to avoid death, but also to maintain life in the highest possible degree of satisfaction. It is the selfish instinct. It would be safe to say that it is basic and that the other instincts work in function of it. It could be identified with Freud's idea of the libido, the pleasure drive.

Race-conservation is more than impulse to procreate. It includes the parental instinct which guards, protects, and forms the young of the

---

[6] W. H. R. Rivers, *Instinct and the Unconscious*, 2nd ed., (New York: Cambridge University Press, 1924).

species. In a broader conception of sex-instinct, parental instinct is contained.

Gregariousness impels us not only to associate with our like, but also to influence the group—at least in the sense of having the group esteem us, at most by dominating the group.

Self conservation and the religious assent

God as a preserver of life and the guarantee of immortality is an object that corresponds to the self-preservation instinct. Immortality can easily be the rationalization of the impulse in all living beings to continue in life.

In the same way the notion of a being on whom the individual or the tribe depends, who can by his power give blessings and avert catastrophes, who provides what is necessary, easily harmonizes with the impulse to have these things. The notion of Divine Providence certainly corresponds to the self-preservation impulse. The correspondence either is a pointer to an objective fact or produces a rationalization of the impulse itself. The harmonious concordance of the theory and the impulse is a fact. The validity of the theory is not proved by the harmony, much less is it denied by it.

One clear instance of man's propensity toward God-assent because of self-preservation is the dictum: There are no atheists in foxholes. Soldiers in the battlefield always show religiosity, even though their religion may seem thin enough when in a peacetime environment. The instinctive element in their battle commitments is very patent. In like manner, men close to nature—sailors, hunters, farmers—always show some religious assent. Atheism is certainly not "natural."

It must be remembered that this instinctive influence in the assent can also be a mere fact of life, and as a fact can be analyzed rationally. In the light of the analysis and given the teleological principle that natural dynamisms are pointers to the reality of the goal of the dynamism, it is possible to make a rational proof from the phenomenon. This has been done, and when it is done, there is ratiocination and not rationalization.

Sex-instinct

In the hey-day of Freudian enthusiasm, when everything below heaven and above it was being explained by libido and sex, the theory was proposed by the Freudian illuminati that religion was a sublimation or perversion of the sex-instinct. In the simplest form, they simply declared that religion was a misinterpretation of libidinous activity. For Freud, God was the Father-image dominating man because of the Oedipus-Complex. Morality was the restriction on the ego superimposed by the Oedipus-Complex. To put it with utmost simplicity, there is no God and there is no objective morality. Today this kind of simplification is avoided. Gregory Zilboorg in his *Mind, Medicine, and Man*[7] has a whole chapter on religion and, though he is Freudian in general tendency, he is most sympathetic to religion and does not deny that typical Freudian thought did not adequately deal with the religious question. Carl Jung in his *Psychology and Religion*[8] certainly favors religion as a valid experience.

The old Freudian position was as follows:

(1) Religious growth is parallel to sex-growth.
(2) Religion expresses itself in terms of eroticism.
(3) Religion is mainly preoccupied with chastity.
(4) Religion always ends up in sex license.

The conclusion is that religion is the sexual in perverted form, or the misinterpretation of sex activity, or at best sublimation.

At least we see in the exposition a definite influence of sex on religion. Let us analyze the observations made.

(1) *Religious growth is parallel to sex-growth.* The proof of this statement is the phenomenon of adolescent conversion. Now Starbuck[9] in his work was interested in adolescent conversion, and because adolescents were the only objects of experiment he restricted his studies to this type of religious behavior. The result was that early psychology of religion was thrust into the examination of adolescent conversion out of all proportion with the importance of the phenomenon.

Adolescent conversion as Starbuck dealt with it, was not a universal phenomenon. Among American non-Catholics of vague or non-existent religious backgrounds the phenomenon is not rare. What is more, it is striking. However, among Catholics trained from childhood, the phenomen is not common. There is an evolution in their religious structure but not a simple conversion from 0 to 10. Adolescence is a time of change, of maturation, and there is no need for surprise that the religious convictions of the child undergo an evolution, but this is hardly true con-

---

[7] New York: Harcourt, Brace & Co., 1943.
[8] New Haven: Yale University Press/London: H. Milford, Oxford University Press, 1938.
[9] Edwin Diller Starbuck, *The Psychology of Religion: an Empirical Study of the Growth of Religious Consciousness*, preface by William James, 3rd ed. (New York: Charles Scribner's Sons, 1911).

version. It may be that the problems of adolescence bring up the religious question to the adolescent which had never been faced before and that as a consequence there may be a conversion, but this is hardly a sexual experience, even though sex considerations may be involved.

Whatever truth there is in the observation that religious growth is parallel to sex growth still leaves the question of dependence open. Sex growth is only one aspect of the growth of the adolescent, and only the supposition that man is essentially a sex dynamism will justify the view that all other growths are functions of libido. This supposition is a postulate whose truth is not proved and which postulate, even though perhaps useful as a therapeutic device, can easily be false. In fact, it seems to be false as a descriptive psychology of the human phenomenon.

That sex-maturity is achieved simultaneously with religious maturity in the maturing period called adolescence is evidently true. That one is the other is an easy hypothesis that shows the signs of oversimplification. That sex-maturation will influence religious-maturation, recognizing the unity of the person, is a priori plausible and in observation generally a fact. This fact no more proves that religion depends on sex than it does that sex depends on religion. It can and should be admitted that the sex-maturation brings with it moral questions and under morality-emotions the individual will take religious stands. But these stands may be negative, as is easily seen in lands of Mediterranean culture. Sex-maturation separates the young people from religion; it does not bind them.

More important than anything is the curve described by religious life in contrast with the sex-curve. As age comes on the individual, the sex curve declines, but there is a tendency of a rise in the religious curve. If the Freudian were right in his explanation of adolescent religiosity, then it would follow that as sex activity wanes, so should religious activity. But this is not true, rather the contrary. The Freudian might answer that this is a compensation, but the compensation theory supposes what was never originally proved. If he wishes to suppose from the beginning that religion is a sex phenomenon, no one can stop him. But supposition is not proof, and is valid only if it increases an understanding of the thing for which the supposition is made. That the Freudian theory of religion helps us understand religion better seems a dubious statement, at least.

(2) That religion can be expressed in erotic terms is a fact. One of the books of the Bible—the *Song of Songs,* or *Canticle of Canticles*—is a series of prothalamial poems and has always enjoyed favor with religious persons. The poems of Saint John of the Cross certainly sound like love poems. The mystics not infrequently use erotic language to describe their

religious experiences, and in some cases this seems to be almost central in their description of the numinous as the beloved. Even in so sober a book as Kempis, Christ is called the Beloved.

However, the most important fact is that this is not the only form of expression for the relationship of numinous and human subject. In fact it is not the most usual one. Theologians are religious persons and a perusal of theological literature will find it singularly poor in erotic terminology. What is more, the majority of religious people do not use erotic terminology in discussing religion, and not a few feel embarrassed when others do use it.

Religion can be expressed in many terminologies. Mythical and legendary forms are common in primitive religions. The language of speculation is used by theologians. In sermons analogies are drawn from patriotism, nature, father-and-son relationship. The favorite prayer of all Christians, considered as model and epitome of Christian prayer, is devoid of sex-terminology and sex-content, unless the Freudian wishes to see a whole Oedipus-Complex in the term, "Our Father." The life of Christ as given in the gospels deals with sex in passing, but with so little preoccupation that it is evident that in his mind the problem was peripheral.

One weakness that besets the Freudians and which they cannot overcome is the necessary supposition that all love is homogeneous and sex-love is its most genuine expression. This supposition is not shared by men at large nor by students of psychology. Sex-love is one form of love and the other forms are experienced freely and widely. Sex-love has one thing in its favor. It is intense and ecstatic, and most people have felt it in this form. The result is that a different kind of love, also intense and ecstatic, would employ love-terminology spontaneously, because that is the kind of terminology at general disposal for such experience. The love-experience of the mystic is not a common thing and it is not shared by the vast majority of men. Hence it has not developed its own terminology and will be forced to use one not its own but analogous to it.

The Freudian, to prove that religion is a sex-phenomenon, would have to show that religion can only be expressed in sex-terms, or at least in fact is expressed exclusively in such terms, and when such terms are used, they are univocal with sex-experience. In the light of facts, it seems that such a task cannot be performed.

(3) All religions inculcate some kind of chastity. The Romans had their Vestal Virgins. The Delphic Pythoness was a virgin. They usually oppose adultery. The Catholic religion prohibits sex-activity to all unless they be married, and for them the activity must be restricted to the part-

ners of the marriage. There have been some religions which forbade absolutely all forms of marriage or sex-activity, as for example, the Shakers, the Essenes. In most religions, there are groups that relinquish even marriage, e.g., Buddhist monks and nuns, Yogi ascetics, Catholic and Orthodox monks and nuns.

However, no vital religion opposed sex-activity altogether. This is a priori evident, for the religion would die in a single generation. The Shakers adopted children, but the Shaker system must be a parasitic growth on a society that does not share their sex-views. In most religions there is no opposition to sex, and in High Anglicanism, Roman Catholicism, and Eastern Orthodoxy, marriage, so far from being condemned, is a sacrament, a holy thing. In fact, celibacy is not sacramental, though marriage is.

The Freudian is in this question betrayed by his own postulates which necessarily make religion a sex-phenomenon. However, postulates are not proofs of fact. The Freudian cannot believe in any objective morality other than the conventions of the group which at most are pragmatically justifiable. For a Freudian no sex-activity is of itself immoral, but rendered so by an Oedipus-Complex tabu. Men at large do not share this point of view. Freudianism believes that the modesty that we find in all cultures concerning sex-activity and sex-phenomena is a repression, and that religion which inculcates modesty is therefore a repression-phenomenon. If we begin our thinking by postulating that all human activity is libidinous, the Freudian position follows in logic. The thing to be analyzed is the validity of the postulate and not the rectitude of the conclusion that follows from it.

What the Freudian on principle cannot admit is that modesty is just as natural as sex-activity. Lack of modesty is always considered as a sign of mental unbalance, and we are not surprised if we find it in psychotics, intoxicated and frenzied persons. Such instances prove that the normal person is modest and expects modesty of other normal persons. Even small children learn modesty very easily. No great effort is needed in such education, though education plays a part.

Nor can the Freudian believe that the libidinous can be controlled. He thinks that it will be used, perverted, or repressed. Control is not repression, any more than a dam represses water, for it only controls it to achieve greater efficiency. Because religion seeks for control in the chaotic and boisterous libidinous activity does not mean that religion is repressing it. It wishes only to introduce order and rationality into it so that it will be human, for after all, human beings do want life to be rational. If the libidinous is not controlled rationally, it will mean the end of society, the end of the individual, and the end of culture. No doubt these are different views as to the demands of reason for the matter of such control, but let us not look at the rational demand for control as a phenomenon of repression.

(4) It is true that sexual licentiousness can be found as a religious phenomenon. In the older religions, religious prostitution was an accepted institution. The Graeco-Roman mysteries were in most instances orgiastic and sexually orgiastic. The American frontier revival often ended in frenzied orgy. Certain Russian heretical sects go in for such practice, and the antinomianism of the old Gnostics opened the door to such behavior, if we believe what their enemies say of them. In South America many religious feasts of a popular nature, involving some days of celebration, will end up in orgy. These things, however, are relics of Indian religion before Christianity came and the Indian has not yet left his old gods and demons altogether.

Even the Freudians admit that this is a non-logical development of religion. They merely think that they see in it the true dynamism at work in all religious activity. However, let us examine the phenomenon.

First, religions which as part of their doctrine include sexual promiscuity as elements of cult usually receive the strong attack of the society where such religion dwells. Such religions rarely have survival value.

Secondly, sexual aberrations that parasitically cling to the fringes of a religion do not constitute elements of that religion and are not a true phenomenon of it. Just because a political convention may include a certain amount of promiscuity, we are hardly justified in considering politics as a sexual phenomenon.

The Freudian must show that religion by inner logic or by continuous historical tradition over the majority of religious persons leads to sexual licentiousness. This goes counter to the facts. Except for some few, minor religions, by theory sexual license is excluded from religion. As an historical fact, the vast majority of religious people do not indulge in sexual license and condemn those who do so in the name of, or on the occasion of, religious activity.

In other words the Freudians have not proved their thesis that religion is a perversion of the sex-instinct. They have, however, proved what was known before: that the sexual instinct influences religious assent. This can be done in various ways.

First, the moral problems raised by sex are solved by religion, and a moral need in this matter may and often does lead a man in terms of morality-emotions to religion. This is probably very common.

Secondly, just as there are people for whom thought activity is the main concern in life and all else peripheral, so there are others for whom sex-activity is the main concern. Sex is central in their existence. Such a person could be religious simultaneously, and his religion will be colored by his sex-interests. There is no injustice to religion to say that deeply religious persons might be so constituted and it will be manifest in their religious life and work. Sex-activity in such persons would not be overt. It would be a tortuous activity latent in other acts. A preoccupation with sex would be manifest in their religious thoughts and messages.

Therefore it is quite possible that we shall find eminently religious persons manifesting sexual energy in their approach to the numinous. Provided that the numinous be not identified with sex and that the thought of the numinous restrict sex-activity to the law of reason, there is nothing illegitimate in such religiosity any more than the religiosity of an intellectual be highly intellectualistic. If, therefore, the psychological analysis of the writings and lives of certain saints shows up a strong sexual tendency, there is no need to deny that it is there. It does not necessarily cancel out the religious. On the other hand we must be cautious in dealing with many modern studies of saints and mystics, where the inspiration of the study is clearly and deliberately Freudian. There is a fierce monomania in Freudianism, and monomania, though quite capable of discovering truths, is rarely capable of discovering the truth.

Gregariousness

The gregarious impulse will certainly have an influence on religious assent. Where a community is bound together by religious beliefs and where admission to the community is impossible without an acceptance of the community's faith, the gregarious will tend to lead men to the assent of the community. What the individual wants is affiliation in the group for instinctive reasons, and the assent will be dictated by the instinct. This does not mean insincerity. It does, however, mean weak religious conviction, and if the community shifts its religious vision, such individuals will shift with no great protest.

This truth will make us understand why a mass conversion is possible and frequent. A sudden mass conversion simply shows that many, if not most of the mass have not considered the problem with due care. (The conversion of the Saxons and the phenomenon of the Japanese in São Paulo.)

There is another phenomenon in religion which manifests the influence of the gregarious instinct. Adolescents in general, and some men all their lives, need a communal cause whose triumph is the first concern. Individual mediocrity is recompensed by group excellence. Corporate pride is quite compatible with individual humility. Gregariousness also includes the power-drive, and any community can be the field of such drives. The Apostles in the Gospel were certainly dedicated to the coming of the Kingdom of God, but they also wished to be the princes in the Kingdom. The ambition of clerics for honors and power in their community is not truly religious, though it certainly is gregarious. The young man who wishes to do big things and be powerful in a given group can readily choose a religious group as the area of his ambitions. It is well to bear this in mind. Many young religious enthusiasts are not religious at all. They want the triumph of their cause and the destruction of the adversaries, but the numinous has nothing to do with the activity. They could just as readily have joined the Communists, and communist or religious, their activity is not dynamized by an idea but by their instinct. The love of strenuous activity of young people, the anxiety to battle with the foe, the very desire of martyrdom for their cause, all are signs of gregariousness and not signs of religion. School spirit is one manifestation of gregariousness and school spirit can easily be substituted by religious sect spirit.

Repression, imposed or chosen, of gregariousness can have a great influence on religious assent. Too little is known concerning the life of Alexander Selkirk on the Island of Juan Fernandez, but Daniel Defoe in his *Robinson Crusoe* shows fine insight into human nature even though he may not have been too faithful to the life of Alexander Selkirk. According to Defoe, Robinson becomes very religious on the island. Gregariousness pushed a man to fellowship, and if no human is about, the numinous becomes attractive or even suggested. The hermits knew this implicitly. They avoided human companionship in order to be thrust onto the divine. Nature-emotions, morality-emotions, and the gregarious through repression can certainly lead a man to the numinous.

As a result of our analysis we can readily admit the influence of instinct on religious assent. Instinct will never dictate such assent, but it can forcefully draw a human being toward such an assent for motives proper to the instinct. In this sense religious assent is instinctive, but instinct neither validates the assent nor does it invalidate it.

The Influence of the Intellect

That intelligence plays a part in religious assent is quite clear from our analysis of the metaphysical answers to the question: how is the numinous achieved? In dealing with the metaphysical treatments of the question we saw two types of answer. One group declared that the numinous was a rationalization of factors of experience, and not a discovery. The other group declared that the numinous was discovered either by a special intellectual process involving intuition, or by the normal use of intellect according to a logical reduction of experience in the light of the first principles of reason. Since our study is epistemological, it is not for us to settle this debate. As a psychological fact it is evident that intellection plays an important part in the forming of the religious assent, which at the very least, will be an intellectual assent, no matter what else it be.

It is merely just that we here make an observation about rationalization which escapes the attention of those who insist that religious assent is always the rationalization of instinct or emotion. The rejection of religion can just as readily be a rationalization as religious assent itself. This is conspicuous in the apostasy of religious people who have fared ill in their religious communities. The young man who has been treated unjustly, or believes that he has been treated unjustly, by a religious group can easily become a belligerent adversary of the vision of that group. Certain types of converts can be explained this way. The young man in a Catholic college fails in his studies. Because of ambition he cannot admit that this failure was caused by lack of intelligence or lack of application. He then explains it by the injustice of the Catholic school, which being a human institution will certainly have instances of injustice to its discredit. The injustice is then used as an argument that proves that all that the Catholic school stands for is false. There then comes a militant crusade against Catholicism. However, when the young man was a Catholic he knew the arguments which he now uses vehemently against Catholicism, and he was not moved by them. They have no intellectual force for him at all. They have no such force for him now. The drive behind his position is thwarted ambition. Rationalization is a two-edged sword. It can be used by anti-religious persons but it can also be used by religious persons against their adversaries.

4

The Epistemological Problem: Mysticism

We cannot end our analysis of religious knowledge without dealing with mysticism. Everytime that we had to face it, we relegated it to a consideration apart. We now shall deal with it summarily.

Mysticism is important for two reasons. First of all, if it is what the mystics pretend it to be, then the numinous can be achieved by immediate experience, requiring neither conceptualization, ratiocination, or rationalization. Secondly, if the mystics be right in their affirmations, then the human intellect has a power which is not sufficiently studied in philosophy and psychology, namely the power of the intuition of an existent which is other than the phenomenal ego.

What are the facts?

There is an abiding tradition in all cultures that some men and women have seen the numinous without the veil of concepts or images, in a personal encounter. In Hebrew literature Moses is supposed to have met Yahweh in this fashion (*Exodus* 33, 17-23). The prophets of the Old Testament, if not mystics, were certainly closely attached to this tradition (*Isaias* 6, 1-8). The Hebrew ascetics, such as the Essenes, certainly were given to more than asceticism and some were given to contemplation (cf. Paul, *Galatians* 1, 11-12, 17) In the Talmudic tradition there are contemplative rabbis. In India yoga has only one purpose, mystical contemplation, and yoga finds its roots in the ancient Vedanta. Buddhism is only a varient of yoga and also tends toward Nirvana contemplation. Among the Moslems the Sufi tradition is a mystical tradition. In Christianity, Catholic, Orthodox and Protestant, the mystical tradition is long and splendid. It begins with Paul (II *Corinthians* 12, 1-7) and includes such names as Saint Francis Assisi, Saint Thomas Aquinas, Meister Eckhardt, Saint Catherine of Sienna, Saint Catherine of Genoa, John of Ruysbroeck, Saint Ignatius of Loyola, Saint Teresa of Avila, Saint John of the Cross, Angela of Foligno, Juliana of Norwich, Saint Therese of Lisieux, and countless others. Among the Protestants must be mentioned Jakob Boehme and Valentine Weigel.

What Mysticism Is Not

There is much literature written by the mystics themselves. They speak a common language though it is quite clear that many write without any dependence, literary or contactual, on the others. For the sake of clarity, we shall rely principally on the *Autobiography* of Saint Teresa of Avila, though this book must be understood in the light of the *Moradas* (Mansions).[1] To our tastes, the best philosophical and psychological study of the whole phenomenon is the work of Père Joseph Maréchal—*Studies in the Psychology of the Mystics*.[2]

There are certain phenomena which are connected with religion which belong to the field of parapsychology, i.e., the study of extraordinary phenomena in human behavior.

(1) *Inspiration*—an impulse to write what has been known, normally or abnormally, in the name of the numinous. It does not necessarily imply a consciousness of the numinal thrust.

(2) *Revelation*—knowledge in terms of images and concepts derived without stimulus from an external natural object and caused by the numinous itself. Such revelations may represent past actions in history (revelations of the Passion of Christ) or future events not yet realized (prophecies).

(3) *Visions*—the presence of images, not stimulated by natural objects, which are symbols of the divine. Saint Thomas considers some objective, e.g., Moses and the Burning Bush, *Exodus* 3, 1-5, or the writing on the wall in the halls of Baltassar, *Daniel* 5, 15-29, but the object seen is produced numinously. For others Saint Thomas holds that they are only mental.

(4) *Mind Reading*—the divinely produced knowledge of the thoughts of others without any manifestation on their part. It is claimed that the Curé d'Ars and Don Bosco had this power with reference to penitents.

---

[1] Saint Teresa of Jesus, *Complete Works,* 3 vols., ed. by E. Allison Peers (New York: Sheed & Ward, 1946).

[2] *Op. cit.* Chapter 2, footnote 3.

(5) *Charismata*—action involving the use of bodily organs but abnormal to them.

(a) *Glossolalia*—"the gift of tongues," consists in uttering words whose meaning is not known to the speaker nor necessarily to the hearers. I *Corinthians* 14, 6-40. In kindred fashion some people speak languages they have never known before.

(b) *Interpretation*—the power to understand words whose meaning was never learned before. I *Corinthians* 14, 1-5.

(c) *Fragrance*—a pleasant odor exudes from a person, but not due to any added scent.

(d) *Glory*—a radiance issues from a person. *Exodus* 34, 29-35; *Matthew* 17, 1-5.

(e) *Perpetual Fast*—a complete abandonment of food for days or years. Saint Catherine of Sienna is cited as an example.

(f) *Living Burial*—interment for days or months without inducing death. Masters of yoga submit to this.

(g) *Stigmata*—the sustaining of wounds like those of Christ. The first known claim was made for Saint Francis of Assisi. The wounds bleed and cause pain but do not fester nor do they cause death nor even inactivity.

(h) *Levitation*—the body is raised from the floor in defiance of gravity. Claims are made both for Christians and yogi.

(i) *Bilocation*—the presence of the same body in two places. Saint Thomas claims that this is impossible, and explains pretended cases as vision.

(j) *Telekinesis*—an action is performed at a distance from the agent.

(k) *Extrasensory Perception*—distant events are perceived by the percipient without a proportionate stimulus from the object.

(l) *Thaumaturgy*—marvelous effects are produced in nature, contrary to the normal laws of natural activity. This includes cures worked suddenly or without medical aids. Such activity is related of holy men of all religions.

Now the meaning of all these phenomena has been subjected to great dispute. Some say that they are mere lies and trickery. Others say that they are subjective illusions accepted in good faith. Others say that they are the products of suggestion or hysteria. Others look for recondite explanations in the natural order, denying anything supernatural about them. Others see in them numinous action and declare them to be preternatural intervention of the divine bursting into history.

Only one thing is clear: not one of these phenomena nor all of them together constitute mysticism. Hence the phenomena do not interest us here, no matter how fascinating they may be. They belong to the field of parapsychology and must be studied by men competent in that field.

What Mysticism Is

Having excluded all parapsychological phenomena from the concept of mysticism, what is left for us to study? A phenomenon reported by many men and women which belongs to the order of knowledge though it carries with it a highly emotional overtone. The questions then arise: what is known and how is it known?

According to the mystics, God is known by immediate spiritual awareness. They describe the experience as the feeling of presence. They do not "see" anything; they "feel." The scene is not one of light necessarily, for often the scene is described as total darkness. No "thing" is conceived.

Perhaps the best analogy is that of the feeling that someone is present in the same room with the subject. Such a presence involves no sight; it involves no physical contact and yet we "know" that someone is there. Of course, in such experiences of presence, the person present does act on the subject: odors, very light sounds, impacts of light so slight that they cannot be achieved clearly. However, in the mystical experience there is absolutely no material action on the part of the perceived presence. Nor must we deny that a certain emotional resonance must be had with the object of presence. Friends develop a great sensitivity and can be aware of each other's presence long before others achieve such awareness. A faint characteristic odor, never clearly catalogued; inflections and intonations, never precisely examined; a foot-fall or the measure of the pace; the rhythm of breathing and the manner of exhaling and inhaling; little eccentricities of gesture and stance—all these things can be sensed by the loving friend, although he is unable to explain how he senses them.

Now the simplest explanation of this experience is to say that it is illusion. A highly emotional state, akin to intoxication, is interpreted as an experience of presence. The difficulty with this explanation is that the mystic rejects it altogether as unworthy and as completely inadequate. A blind man could without doubt declare that no one sees, for hallucination is for him the best explanation of an experience he has never had and cannot even imagine. H. G. Wells has a tale concerning a community of blind men who refuse to entertain the notion that anyone can see. This can be the position of those students of the phenomenon who a priori cannot admit any such experience by erecting their lack of experience into a general law which states that no experience of an order not shared by them is objective. Such students are incapable of studying the mystical encounter because they refuse to examine it humbly and with docile attention to those who have had the experience. Many mystics have been quiet, sober, and sensible men and women, with no eccentricities of conduct and behavior. Their testimony would be accepted on events homogeneous with the experience of other men; why are they to be labeled as intoxicated on this experience which meant so much to them? If you declare the mystic's experience impossible by some a priori postulate, there is no need to study his testimony. You know in advance that it will not give you an objective awareness of something that does not fall into natural categories.

Récéjac has another explanation.[3] The mystic begins with an image of high symbolic content, and the concentration on this image produces an exquisite emotional state, even to the point of fainting. Now the difficulty with this explanation is that the mystic insists that he was aware of something which he cannot express by image or by concept. It was this awareness that was gripping, not merely the state following upon reflection on the object of awareness. The state of the mystic is essentially an awareness state and not emotional, though the emotional consequent is also there.

Many psychologists make the mistake of Récéjac but in cruder form. They describe the mystical experience as essentially and centrally emotional. They compare it to the luminous moment of the epileptic as he falls into his fit. However, the mystic is not primarily interested in the emotional state, sweet as he finds it. The encounter in terms of awareness of something met is for him the important element. Récéjac and the others reduce mystical experience to an emotional state following on monoideism or image-concentration. Saint Teresa knew what such states were. Her prayer of simplicity is precisely the monoideic reflection, but she says that mystical prayer is totally different.

The only adequate understanding of the mystic's experience, the understanding which a docile reading of his testimony can give, provided no a priori postulate be put in the way, is that the mystic has intuited a reality without image and without concept. Such an intuition is not in analogy with sight but with the analogy of present feeling. There is no image; there is no concept; there is no reduction to categories; there is no judgment; there is only awareness experience and that is intuition.

---

[3] E. Récéjac, *Essay on the Bases of Mystic Knowledge*, trans. by S. C. Upton (New York: Charles Scribner, 1899).

The emotional consequent will undoubtedly be very high, but it was not this which was the important element, though clearly it was the factor that made the experience so desirable.

The Mystical Steps

The preparation

All mystics of all religions insist on a preparation. The end pursued in this preparation is purification. It consists in detaching the person from the attractions of material goods. The yogi insist on complete chastity and complete poverty as the first step. Ambition in all its forms is next excluded. Complete indifference to physical pain is then induced, and it is brought about by the voluntary bearing of pain produced by the ascetic himself. At the same time recollection is sought, i.e., a shutting-out of the world and its turmoil, so that the spirit be quite free to search for the numinous without distraction. Prayer, mental, is the constant activity of the mystic.

Christian mystics also demand this ascetical preparation with a difference. The Orientals think that the preparation will inevitably produce the mystical experience and that anyone can have it, if only he prepares himself for it. The Christians do not believe this. They think that the experience is a free gift which cannot be achieved by human endeavor. What is more, for the Christians the preparation itself is a work of God. He can shorten or lengthen it. He need not follow the yogi pattern but can achieve the end of the yogi asceticism immediately. We never know why he does it, and the only explanation is his good pleasure. Some Catholics, the Dominican School, believe that all Christians are called to the Mystical State and only a defect of the will prevents Christians from achieving it. Saint Teresa seems to be of the same opinion, though at times she speaks ambiguously. The Jesuit School teaches that the mystical grace is not for all, but for those chosen without any merit of their own. As a matter of fact, the two views can be reconciled. Christian grace is something to be developed, and it is in itself the beginning of the Beatific Vision. Hence to all Christians there is given a remote call to the Mystical State, but a proximate call is not given to all. This call depends on the free choice of God.

One element in the preparation is the Dark Night of the Soul. Sadness, weariness, desolation are part of the preparation whereby the soul is rendered detached from all things material. These are trials sent by God according to the Christians, but only the inevitable resistance of the body according to the yogi. The Dark Night does not disappear at the arrival of the first mystical stage, but each stage has its own preparation and the trials and tribulations of the spirit continue throughout his growth.

Some psychologists discuss the problem whether some kind of pathological condition is necessary for the mystical experience. Those who think that it is required, suppose that an abnormal sensitivity, which is necessary for the mystical perception, means a pathological psyche. Others deny this, and insist that mysticism is not a pathological condition, nor a consequent on pathological conditions, but that it is an experience of a psyche in greatest health.

The prayer of quiet

In her description of prayer, Teresa compares different forms of prayer to the watering of a garden. In discursive prayer, the subject goes to a well with a bucket, fills it, and carries it to the plants. In the prayer of simplicity, which for Teresa is the prayer required in the state of preparation for the mystical experience, pipes are placed bringing the water to the plants. However, there soon comes a form of prayer totally different from the prayer of simplicity which is only a suggestion phenomenon. In this new prayer, the plants are watered by the overflow of the spring.

In this new prayer the whole experience is different. There is an area of the intellect which does not deal with concepts. It feels the presence of God but there are concepts and images simultaneously which distract the mind and bewilder it. It is like the condition of a man who sees a jewel in a confusion of buttons but cannot concentrate on it, although he does see it. The emotional accompaniment is high and gratifying but mixed with the attraction of the buttons. It is a confused perception of presence and a confused state of joy.

At first this state is of short duration but later it may last for hours. Bodily movement is not lost and the contemplative may be in motion, though excessive movement will end the state. Sensations are experienced. Contact with the outer world remains intact, though the contemplative seems in a state of bewilderment and absent-mindedness.

The prayer of union

The mystic is highly pleased with the prayer of quiet, but he longs for a more satisfying perception of the numinous. He wishes to see without distraction. If the growth goes on, he will reach the prayer of Union. In essence this prayer is not different from the previous one, but only a more perfect instance. There are no thoughts, no images, no possibility of voluntary thinking processes. The confused perception of the previous prayer now disappears and the mind is exclusively concentrated on the numinous which it perceives with no concepts and with no images. There is no judgment and no inferential thinking processes. The joy is very intense and fills the person. There is no distraction of images and concepts. It is a fruition of the union attained.

However, contact with the outer world is not wholly lost. There is sensation but so peripheral that it does not fall within the line of attention. There can still be voluntary bodily movements, but there is little movement, and movement will end the experience. By reason of this thin connection with the outer world, the person can be called from the contemplation and the state be lost. Mystics are not clear as to the length of the state. According to Saint Teresa, it is short.

Both this prayer as well as the preceding and the following can come suddenly and without immediate preparation, though normally they are transition states in ordinary prayer. Yet at times they fall on the mystic when engaged in work or bodily activity. Willing can neither produce it nor end it. The will as a striving is inactive.

Ecstasy

This is the high point of the mystic's experience. The perception of the numinous is now at its most intense. The whole attention of the contemplative is on the numinous perceived within the nucleus of the mind. Now no distractions are possible. There are no concepts, no images, no other awareness than of the numinous. Even the peripheral awareness of sensation is dead, and the will is inert as a dynamism to action. The will only acts in complacence and rapturous joy. The exclusion of all awareness other than that of the numinous is brought about by a trance, so that the body goes into something like a cataleptic fit— the ecstasy, the being outside of onself; the rapture, the being taken elsewhere. The cataleptic trance does not produce rigidity of the body, but there is a slowing of the heart-beat and of the pulse; at times to the point where there seems to be no pulse at all. However, the contemplative can be aroused from the trance by someone stirring the body, but the mystic himself cannot produce this movement.

It must be insisted that this is not a state of unconsciousness. The mystic is not only fully conscious but awareness is most acute, but pleasurably acute.

This is the great experience of the mystic and he longs for it once he has had it. However, all masters of mystical prayer warn over and over again that it must not be sought for because of its emotional richness. Once the rapture has been attained, it comes again. It is rarely restricted to a single instance.

Saint Teresa speaks ambiguously about the length of the experience. She says in one place that it is short and in other places that it is long. There can be a reconciliation of the statements. The total experience—going into the trance and coming out—may be long, but the acute awareness which is the high point of the contemplation, may be quite short. This is quite plausible because the vision is overcoming.

Spiritual Nuptials

When the mystic has reached the full growth of his state, the experience differs totally. All the previous states have been states of introversion and fleeing from the world and worldly activity. In the last stage, Spiritual Nuptials, the mystic turns outwards and performs unbelievable feats of creativity. Ecstasy is rare if present at all; it is not desired. In place of acute awareness of the numinous which is rapturous, there comes an abiding awareness of the numinous, calm, unruffled, and stable. Not only is the mystic aware of God, but also aware of himself as God's instrument. There is now self-consciousness embedded in God-consciousness, but the two agents are united. The mystic now acts for God and with God. There is tireless effort but complete peace. The mystic knows that he is in God's hands, doing God's work, and cannot be foiled. Obstacles do not worry him, for he knows that they will be overcome. Some mystics speak of this activity as automatic, i.e., not willed. Saint Teresa, however, makes it clear that it is willed activity.

In this state which lasts till the end of life, the mystic deals with things and people. Saint Teresa, overcoming much opposition, built some forty monasteries. Saint Catherine of Sienna went on long voyages and dealt with all kinds of people. In spite of this tremendous activity, there is perfect peace in the soul of the mystic. We have here the image of Saint Thomas working out. He wanted the Christian to fill his soul with God by contemplation until the precious liquor overflowed to the neighbor. The Spiritual Nuptials—an abiding union—is the overflowing of God, constant and peaceful.

This last stage of mysticism explains the whole nature of the phenomenon. The dynamism of mystical experience is not the seclusion of the mystic from life and activity, though the initial stages do produce such a seclusion. However, this segregation is preparatory for a total transformation of the mystic. The mystical experience wishes to transform the mystic altogether. When the transformation is complete, then the activity comes into play. The whole range of mysticism is the absorption of the contemplative *into God*. When this absorption is achieved, then numinous action is demanded of the mystic and he joyfully accepts. Action now is not in terms of instinct or ambition, but in function of the divine will. The mystic is always in contact with that will and allows himself freely to be directed by it exclusively. Creativity is heightened and creativity is logical and continuous. It is, moreover, true creativity; the action of God in an instrument united to Him intimately, awarely and lovingly. Martha and Mary blend into one agent.

Conclusion

Mysticism is not a widespread experience, but it is sufficiently frequent so as to be impressive. No one denies that the mystical experience is a fact. There is, however, no agreement as to the nature of the phenomenon.

A naturalist explanation is certainly conceivable. After all, mysticism takes place in history which has a naturalistic setting. However, a naturalistic explanation must always suppose that the mystic is deluded and that we should not believe him when he says that he has met the numinous in an intuitive encounter. This makes a strange explanation. We accept the testimony of the mystic for everything except the central point of his testimony. He insists that he has met God, and the naturalist says that here he is mistaken, though in all else, that which is secondary as far as the mystic is concerned, he can be trusted. This kind of pick-and-choose method of examination seems most arbitrary. After all, it is evident that I cannot tell the mystic what he has experienced, if I do not know what his experience is. There is no law that says that his experience must be homogeneous with mine, where the mystical does not show up. This is all the more true because the mystic insists that this experience is different from normal experiences and to reduce it to the normal is to deny the whole phenomenon. The farmer who at the sight of a giraffe cried, "There ain't no such animal," was not loyal to the data. Reality is not bound to a system of categories applicable to one restricted mode of life and interest.

Even Catholic philosophers are not too loyal to the data. Saint Thomas states that rapture is knowledge without concepts and yet Billuart in a footnote to the passage says that the Doctor cannot mean this, for all knowledge is in terms of abstraction, which is a rather smug way of solving the problem of knowledge. A framework erected to explain one field of phenomena is made universal, even for phenomena beyond the field originally examined.

Nihil in intellectu quod non prius in sensu[4] is a principle achieved empirically and not metaphysically. It is not valid except for that area of knowledge which indicates empirical content of the natural order. Even in that order the principle is not as universal as it wishes to be. To quote the principle in the case of mystical knowledge is simply beside the point, or so to understand the principle that it is a truism with its precise meaning washed out.

----

[4] There is nothing in the intellect which was not previously in the senses.

5

Epistemological Consequences of the Religious Experience

The Relevance of Religion

There has been a tradition in philosophy to ignore religious experience in dealing with the epistemological question. In terms of history this is intelligible enough. Aristotle had no proper concept of the religious, and Plato's religion is a matter of dispute. For the classical philosophic mind, religion was a phenomenon it did not think worthy of consideration. In some this position implied piety, for they thought that the religious was on a plane superior to philosophy and therefore it would have been sacrilegious to treat it philosophically. These men had too humble a view concerning philosophy. Others considered religion a thing of emotion with no rational structure at all, and they considered religion an unworthy theme of philosophy. They had too low an estimate of religion.

Plotinus and the Neo-Platonists reduced philosophy to religion and made knowledge mysticism. This transformation pleased the Fathers of the Church, but it was cruel to philosophy. It was Aquinas who quite probably felt the influence, even if indirectly, of Abelard, and wished to secure for philosophy its independent field of sovereignty. In doing so, he made philosophy natural, and religion supernatural, whose intellectual discipline would be theology.

Aquinas did what had to be done, but giving the natural to philosophy does not necessarily make philosophy naturalism, nor was such the intention of Aquinas. Nor do we do justice to the mind of Saint Thomas by

79

saying that philosophy must recognize the supernatural because theology is its negative norm.

Natural and supernatural are metaphysical terms. They are not psychological terms nor even epistemological terms. If by "nature" we mean history, then all that we can say is that the natural would not exclude the supernatural. History a priori could be shot through with the supernatural, and in terms of the commitments of faith, it is so shot through.

Epistemology does not begin with metaphysics. It implicitly posits a metaphysics but it is essentially the reduction of an historical phenomenon to unity and economy. The phenomenon is the psychological activity we call knowing. This phenomenon is, therefore, psychological and historical. On this level the words "natural" and "supernatural" are meaningless. If in the data of psychology and history the supernatural is included, the supernatural must play a part in epistemology, and the arbitrary exclusion of it, will work havoc with the epistemological effort. This has happened.

The great contribution of Edmund Husserl was the discovery of the phenomenological method. Philosophy must deal with problems as given in experience. There is a prime datum and this is accepted. It cannot not be accepted, for it is imperiously given. The datum is not given as a blind element in chaotic experience but as meaningful. Datum and meaning are given simultaneously. In Thomistic terminology, existence and essence are given in any being. One cannot go beyond meaning and one cannot evacuate meanings out of phenomenological examination, though one can restrict the area of phenomenological research.

If epistemology wishes to use the phenomenological method—and what other method can it use?—then the phenomenon that it must consider is the thinking process. It will not be a true epistemology unless it examines all thinking. Religious thinking is a phenomenon and thus it must play an important part in the epistemological enterprise, precisely because it shows characteristics different from those of other types of thinking.

This type of consideration will prove irksome to many philosophers, even those not adverse to religion. They find that the religious question just obfuscates the epistemological problem. They prefer therefore to eliminate it from their considerations. This tendency is understandable, but we must protest against it in the name of philosophy. It is easy to deal with problems if we ignore all the vexing elements of the problem. What is worse, when a scheme is erected, ignoring the vexing elements, and these elements are then examined by the scheme, if they do not fit into the scheme, they are declared to be unreal. This is a vicious method.

You ignore certain phases of the problem, and then solve such phases by a theory erected as a consequence of the original ignoring. You refuse to consider the baby in the bath, and then declare the baby is not there because your analysis of the bath-water shows no baby elements. It is not surprising that the baby will be allowed to go down the drain with the bath-water.

Nor can we sympathize with those who insist that all such problems should be treated by theology. The religious is not only a datum of revelation; it is also an element in the historical phenomenon called man. As a phenomenon it can be studied phenomenologically, and such a study is not theology. We do no injustice to the religious phenomenon by studying it in the psychology of religion, though such a study is neither metaphysical nor theological. That the psychological does not give metaphysical answers is obvious enough. That it will, therefore, give no last answers is also obvious, but religion is a psychological phenomenon and can be treated in the descriptive science that deals with conscious phenomena. Anyone who thinks that this kind of study is the only one possible is speaking metaphysically. Such a thought does not derive from his psychological work but from a metaphysical postulate. A very sick man can be an excellent doctor, and an excellent doctor can be a very poor metaphysician.

Therefore no espitemological theory can ignore the problem of religious assent. Nor can an epistemology be erected without taking this assent as one of the most fascinating forms of human knowledge. As epistemologists we must protest against the arbitrary exclusion of religious knowledge from epistemological consideration. This does not mean that epistemology should deal with religion *after* it has erected its own scheme whose structure totally ignored the religious fact. Religion must be considered before any scheme is confected.

The Absolute and the Numinous

All philosophies will develop a metaphysics. The philosopher who tries to keep away from this task is deluding himself. He is trying to build an edifice without the first floor. Every attack on metaphysics is not a real attack on metaphysics, but a metaphysical attack on this or that metaphysics. Philosophy tries to organize thinking into a unity and there will be a number one from which it must proceed. This will be the philosophic absolute. It does not have to be personified, but it must be recognized. Aristotle had his Prime Mover and Plato his Highest

Good. The materialist has an all sufficient matter, eternal and indestruct-
ible, while his more sophisticated successor, the naturalist, has his Nature.

The act peculiar to religion is prayer. The object of this prayer is the
numinous. In some sense or other it must be personified, because we
cannot pray to impersonality. Now the absolute of philosophy cannot be
the object of prayer. It is the prius of all thought and as a priority to
thought it functions in thought. Thinking is not praying, although
praying supposes thinking. The numinous cannot be distinct from the
Absolute but it is recognized differently. It is the great First, utterly
independent, on which all else depends, mysterious, awesome, fascinating,
capable of being met in a vital encounter, but incapable of being hedged
in by humanly set boundaries. It is met in human experience but not on
the plane of human experience.

Now philosophy cannot escape the Absolute, for it is a quest for the
Absolute. Philosophy must escape the numinous as object, because the
numinous as object is met in religion and not in philosophy. But, the
religious meeting is real, at least as a phenomenon of human experience.
Philosophy cannot ignore this meeting, this reality. It cannot do justice
to it, for it always deals with it as absolute and not numinous. Just
because it cannot do justice to it does not mean that it does injustice.
A partial aspect is not the same as no aspect at all.

One branch of philosophy meets the numinous as numinous and that
is epistemology. Since it deals with all thinking, it also must deal with the
peculiar thinking whereby the numinous swims into our ken. It meets
it as it meets all thought—namely as thought, and not as the object of
thought. A metaphysic will criticize the validity of the thought in the
light of a study of the object as given in thought. A metaphysic will
compare the object with its own notion of being, and consider it real
or unreal in the light of that initial notion. However, epistemology
cannot make such a criticism. It cannot in its own right declare the
thought of the numinous to be an illusion, a useful reconstruction of
the philosophic absolute, or real as conceived. Epistemology can reject
the numinous only if the numinous contradicts the notion of knowledge
or is not logically assimilable. If there is no contradiction of the epistemological task nor a logical contradiction, epistemology must not
only accept the numinous as thought but also as a manifestation of the
capacities of thought. If metaphysically the numinous is acceptable,
epistemology must grant humbly to thought its acquisition of the numinous. Epistemology defends perception; it does not try to restrict it or
question it. Perception is imperious, and epistemology and logic control
perception only in as far as they must exclude as perception that which

makes perception inconsistent with itself, i.e., makes of perception non-perception.

Epistemological Investigations

Let us state some metaphysical principles which are guiding this research.

(1) *There is an absolute.* No philosopher will deny this proposition. If he tries to do so, he falls into nothingness, which puts him beyond philosophy which deals with the real in its most general aspects. The real must in its nucleus be absolute, for if not, reality would be exclusively relative. Relations however cannot be thought unless they are references to the absolute. Relation is reference. It points to somthing beyond itself, and though there can be relations of relations, yet the first relation must point to something not relative, for otherwise it could not be thought of.

Much has been spoken about the nature of the absolute. These discussions only underline the universal acceptance of some kind of absolute. The doubt does not arise concerning the *Dasein* of the absolute, but only concerning its *Sosein*.

(2) *Nothing prevents the absolute from being numinous.* The absolute is the prius of all thought. As absolute it is not experienced, since it is prior to experience. It is metempirical. There is nothing in such a notion that will prevent the absolute from being more than thought-ultimate. In fact it must be the reality-ultimate. Since it precedes all categorization, it lies beyond the categories, and these cannot be invoked to limit it. Consequently, as a reality-ultimate it can be capable of personal encounter. Even as thought-ultimate it will be totally other, the source of all relatives which are meaningful only by reference to it, and the unlimited being, because unrelated. Even personality is granted to it as a thought-absolute, for personality is found in experience and is relative or absolute. Absolute personality is identical with the philosophic absolute, for two absolutes are inconceivable, since being two of the same kind they are related to each other by the relation of similarity, and so the unrelated absolute must be one. This philosophic personality, the capacity of thought and willing, is quite a different thing from the personality that we meet in encounter, though it is the thought-basis of experienced personality. The personal absolute of philosophy is not the same as the personal numinous of religion, though in reality there is no difference. Philosophy deals with the personal absolute as he is presented

in thought. Religion deals with the numinous as the Other of encounter. There are no existent commitments in the recognition that the thought-absolute is personal, though such a notion would lead the human subject to consider the object of thought in a vital way and of ultimate human concern. The vital concern is not philosophic. Philosophy is essentially unconcerned.

(3) *The numinous can be discovered as numinous because of the philosophic analysis of the absolute, given as the prius of experience.* Reality is the measure of thought, and no thought is valid except in so far as it is the acquisition of the real. Thought is not meaningful except in terms of the real which it supposes it reaches. You cannot think unless you think of *something*. A thinker without something thought is nonsense.

Therefore the notion of a prius to thought necessarily puts that prius in reality. Human reference to that reality will engender human concern and thus there is a numinous relationship between man and his thought-absolute. Just how this relationship will work out in man's thought and works is difficult to say. We have no instance in history where the relationship—religion—was worked out except in terms of a supposed revelation, i.e., an action of the numinous on the historic consciousness of man. "Natural religion" therefore is not something that we have met in history. It can only be the object of speculation. Such speculation is not out of place, but it is most difficult to control.

Conclusion

The first problem that faces epistemology as the result of the numinous influence in life is the unescapable conclusion of the fact of knowledge. How can we know an object which is given in thought but not given in experience? There is no room for a discussion of the problem: can a non-empirical object be known? There was Kant's fundamental error. He believed that a non-empirical object could not be known though it could validly be postulated. The Kantian position was possible only in a day when empiricism was successfully challenging rationalism. The answer of course is that the non-empirical cannot be discovered empirically and therefore if "known" means "empirically known," then it is a truism that the non-empirical cannot be "known." However, to reduce knowledge to empiricism is to restrict knowledge to the least important of its activities. Any kind of knowledge involves the prius of knowledge, and that prius can be detected in knowledge and is itself an object of true knowledge, for if it were not, then the whole knowledge process would be fallacious, which is another way of saying that knowledge is a delusion. This type of thinking makes epistemology impossible, for it makes delusion examine delusion—a task that loses all seriousness and which will not be undertaken seriously by anyone. The only epistemological supposition possible is that knowledge is not delusion and that it really does what it pretends, namely give me the real and not illusion.

The answer to the epistemological problem, how can we know an object given in thought but not by experience, requires a number of constellar elements. *First,* we must deny that empiricism is absolute, i.e., the restriction of knowledge to empirical objects. This does not mean that we deny such a thing as empirical knowledge but we must deny that that is all the knowledge there is.

An equivocation must be avoided. The word "experience" is used so loosely today. Of itself it merely means modification of a subject by an object. In philosophy it meant the awareness of object so that awareness is active in its conquest. It later meant the stream of activity as present to awareness. Last of all it meant objective reality in terms of its relationship to an awareful subject and was thus the totality of historical reality, i.e., man's world as evident to man. In the empirical postulate, this was never the world in itself but only the world as humanly interesting and in terms of human interest as found in individuals conditioned by physical constitution and historical *Mitsein.*[1]

All and any knowledge is an act of awareness. As such, all knowledge is an experience and only in experience can knowledge be found. All objects are known in as far as they are interesting to the knower and in terms of his conditioning. In other words, all knowledge is a part of history. Consequently, knowledge always is impure in man, i.e., time and affectivity modify it. It does not exist in a pure state, i.e., an awareness that divests the object of affective and sociological relations. However, this is a far cry from saying that the object of human knowledge is not the object in itself but only the object of human individual concern, an object which clearly is subjective. In spite of the affective and sociological elements in the awareness of objects, the dynamism of the knowledge process is toward the object in itself, for only it is the measure of knowledge. Knowledge is not a human device to satisfy human wishes but an activity to achieve the real, and the real is not identical with the knowing subject, for self-knowledge is only one kind of knowledge. A free agent who is not creative of his willed objects must meet will in terms of the real, and knowledge therefore is prior to his willing, though willing and

---

[1] *Mitsein:* being with others, the social environment and culture.

knowing will have dynamic quests by structure and not by willing as an act. Dynamic impulse must not be confounded with willed impulse. Willed impulse manifests dynamic impulse but not all dynamic impulse is willed impulse. Hence dynamic satisfaction must not be confounded with will-satisfaction.

All knowledge, therefore, reaches the thing-in-itself, but it does not achieve it in its purity ever. Sociological and affective conditioning are the prisms through which the object is seen. However, this refraction does not annihilate the thing-in-itself but only distorts it. It is the task of the philosopher to correct the distortion as far as he can, though he will never eliminate it entirely, and his sincerest efforts at rectifying it may only produce greater distortion. A subsequent age can always recognize the distortion of a past age, but it cannot recognize its own.

Therefore, although it is admitted that we know only in terms of experience, though it is admitted that experience is distortive, though it is admitted that no object can be known except as interesting, though it is admitted that an unknown object as far as man is concerned is practically equivalent to unreality, yet we must admit that we know objects in themselves. We can know such objects even though we have not had any contact with them in terms of mutual friction. The impurity of knowledge does not render knowledge to a state of non-knowledge, to the state of being a will-device to make willing more satisfactory.

Second, the absolute is not merely a postulate of moral endeavor as Kant wished it, but a prius in knowledge itself. A prius is not the same as a postulate. A prius is given along with the object achieved in experience. It is not given as a thing visioned, but as an object related to the thing visioned. Metaphysical analysis can detect the relationship. In other words a natural theology is quite possible, even though it will not reveal the numinous *qua* numinous but merely as a thought-absolute.

Third, a thought-absolute can arouse man to a valid construction of the numinous. This construction will be in terms of analogy, for it is never a univocal grasp of the numinous, yet it is a valid effort in terms of the objective order and can be the basis of human action and commitment. There is a hazard in such construction and by itself it can easily be subject to substantial distortion. There is a moral impossibility that an adequate scheme of numinous reality will be achieved by mere natural thinking. However, a moral impossibility is not the same as a physical impossibility. The moral impossibility derives from the affective and sociological elements that affect knowledge on the human plane.

This is quite clear in Saint Thomas, who can be very luminous in little phrases. In *S.T.*,1,2,3,c. he gives the reduction of the notion of change to an absolute which does not change and he reaches the Aristotelian Prime Mover Unmoved. This is a thought-absolute. Aquinas then proceeds: "and this everyone understands to be God." Prime Mover does not say God, but as Thomas puts it, given such a notion, men will immediately identify it with God. If man had no notion of the numinous, the absolute would suggest it; if they have a notion, they will recognize at once that the absolute corresponds to the notion of the numinous.

The modern impatience with natural theology understands one thing clearly; thought-absolute is not the numinous, and the development of the notion of thought-absolute is not the same as the development of the notion of the numinous. This same impatience does not see another thing which is also there, namely that, given the thought-absolute, man immediately connects it with the numinous which could be achieved just by reflecting on the thought-absolute. The absolute-being thought, and therefore contemplative and detached, involves no commitment. However, in a human being who is more than thought, this very thought will arouse a vision of the numinous that does involve commitment. The modern impatience is in root contemptuous of thought, and refuses to give it any autonomy by subjecting it to the will. Thought is autonomous, though its autonomy is hardly despotic. It is neither absolute lord nor groveling slave. It is clearly carried along by will but never so that it obeys the will blindly. It moves along still retaining its own dignity and basic autonomy.

Fourth, the reality of the numinous, evident or postulated, throws a whole new light on knowledge. His action is possible in knowledge, and that action will not be achievable by reflection. Providence and grace which are non-conscious factors in human activity are not to be cavalierly dismissed as irrelevant to epistemological considerations just because they are not directly perceptible. It is true that the epistemologist, because he cannot find these elements, must not talk about them, but he must not talk as if they were not there and could not be there. His findings must leave open a large area of his scheme so that these things if present are not deprived of the actual role that they actually play. The epistemologist cannot talk of grace, because he has no right to do so, but he must not talk as if his lack of right deprives grace of its rights.

Fifth, neither epistemology nor metaphysics can restrict the numinous in any way. Towards the numinous man can only have the attitude of docility and humility. Neither man's will nor man's intellect can dictate to him. To say a priori that God cannot reveal himself through and in history, not only by the structure of history but by the intrusion of the numinous *qua* numinous, is a proud stand that smacks fearfully of *hybris,* the unforgiveable sin according to Greek thought. If, therefore, history shows or seems to show that the numinous did break through in order that men might know him better and more personally, it is not for epistemology to ignore or deny such a possibility. If history subsequent to a divine break-through carries the task of making men know God in terms of the break-through, epistemology must study the function and nature of the historical communication of truth.

Men know that history communicates truth. It communicates falsehood as well, but this latter fact does not cancel out the former. Epistemology, because of its Cartesian birth, scorned for a long time the whole question of testimony. Yet this road to knowledge is the most used by men. Consequently the lack of consideration of this kind of knowledge in epistemology is lamentable. It is high time that there be an epistemology of testimony and witness, which for the time being has been developed exclusively by jurisprudence and historical methodology.

An epistemology of testimony would not be complete unless it also examined the possibilities and nature of testimony to a numinous break-through. Something like this was done by Catholic theology both in its analysis of faith and in its apologetic task of showing the reasonability of faith, but the essay was not sufficiently phenomenological.

Sixth, man's assent to propositions communicated by history cannot be like the assent imperiously dictated by the intuition of existence or the intuition of meaning, which latter bases the whole logical process. The object grasped in an historical proposition is not experienced by the man who makes the assent. It is an assent made on experience, but the experience of some one else. How can a man assent because of an experience he never had? This is a true epistemological problem and epistemology must answer it. If epistemology tries to answer by saying that such assent is impossible, then epistemology flies into the face of the human phenomenon. Men do make such assents and these assents are the vast majority of those he does make. If epistemology admits that such assents are inevitable but none the less illegitimate, then epistemology finds itself at complete variance with the convictions of human beings. This is hardly justified, for the epistemologist does not know more than men at large, he only organizes this knowledge into an harmonious and economic system.

The answer of course is that the assent to historical testimony is different from the assent of immediate experience involving basic intuitions. My belief in the Battle of Waterloo is totally different from my belief in the proposition that a triangle has three sides. I can see that I cannot be wrong in this latter assent, but I cannot see this with reference to my assent to the reality of the Battle of Waterloo. As far as I can see, my total experience is not contradicted in any detail if I suppose that there never was a Battle of Waterloo. My individual experience does not dictate assent to the reality of Waterloo. However, my own experience leads me to believe that it is not the sum total of all experience and in the fuller experience Waterloo may be demanded. If my own personal experience shows up elements which can only be consistently experienced on the hypothesis of the reality of Waterloo, I accept that hypothesis spontaneously and with no fear. Nor do I accept it as an hypothesis in terms of a functional postulate. I accept it as true. Such an assent is not reasoned but I find it reasonable. It fits with all that reason and experience tell me. This fittingness gives me peace in my assent.

Fittingness is a strange phenomenon. No one denies that there is such a reality but it is hard to control it in thought. Fittingness is affirmed in terms of prudence more than in terms of vision. It is a prudential assent involving will, for fittingness is a good as well as a truth, and its truth is that it is good.

Prudential assent is quite as satisfactory to man as dictated assent. The satisfaction is of a different order, but it is natural satisfaction. With it man is at peace and rest with reference to his own activity. It is clear that prudential assent to historical truth not experienced by the assenter is not capable of ruling out the possibility of the contradictory, but in spite of this impossibility no normal man refuses to make such assents serenely.

On the hypothesis that the numinous broke through into history, the problem of testimony is basically the same for this even as for any other event. Nor can the individual say that in this instance he must refuse to give prudential assent because the commitment is so much greater than in other assents of this order. It is just as prudent to make this assent as any other of its kind, neither more nor less. There is a lack of docility on the part of man to make such a stand with reference to the numinous. He cannot say: you must not do it in this way. That is something that man can never say to the numinous. He must accept the numinous and must accept him on the terms of the numinous and not on his own.

One of the difficulties that seems to vex dialectical theologians is that they so stress the otherness of the numinous that they deny him all possibility of materialization. The notion of the Incarnation of God seems to them impossible and blasphemous. Again we find man putting down terms to God. The dialectical theologians insist so eloquently that no human categories can be used to restrict the being and activity of the numinous and then promptly assure us dogmatically that the numinous

cannot be in any sense materialized. Not only do they commit here a
sin against their own valid principle, but their whole enterprise is a
contradiction. Man according to them knows God in some way. Such
a knowledge involves the materialization of God in some fashion on two
planes. In an historical experience they know God, and thus they
implicitly affirm that God is in material history. Secondly, the knowledge
itself is the possession of a material agent, man, and in that knowledge
God is, in some way. It is impossible for any epistemologist, be his epistemology philosophical or theological, to deny some kind of materialization of God, for God is known in this material world and by a material
thinker.

The real difficulty lies not with the vehement arbitrariness of a man
like Karl Barth but rather with the historical method as conceived by
Von Ranke and Mommsen in the last century. The method of any science
belongs to the realm of logic and not to the realm of epistemology. The
scientist must set up for discipline a method that will make his work
controllable and confined. However, the historical method as we know
it was constructed to deal with historical investigation on all levels but
one. The contrivers of the method did not entertain the thought that
the numinous could break through into history. If they entertained it
even briefly, they decided that it was safer not to deal with it. Such
humility is not out of place and was even justified by producing a splendid
tool for historical investigation where the numinous was not involved.
However, we must protest when we are soberly told that a divine break-
through in history cannot be proved by historical method. If such an
affirmation merely means that the method formed is not capable of
dealing with an investigation of the numinous in history, no harm is
done. It is a mere statement of fact. However, in the mouths of those who
make the affirmation much more is implied. They wish to say that the
break-through of the numinous into history cannot be reasonably ascer-
tained at all. This is affirming elements beyond the true content of the
proposition.

A conquest of the numinous as appearing on the historical scene
involves some elements different from those presented by other historical
events. If the numinous breaks through to an observer not gifted by an
intuition of the numinous, then the divine must show its divinity in the
historical action. That is not a merely natural action, for it is the action
of the supernatural. Of course it will be the supernatural materialized,
but it will not lose thereby all the characteristics proper to the divine.
Such divine characteristics will make the action miraculous, i.e., wonder-
ful and awful and productive of admiration. Historical method has ruled

the miraculous out of its consideration and has even made the historian explain the miraculous as if it were natural. This is treason to the real, a great sin in a man who professes to dedicate himself to the search of the real. Human beings have no fear of the miraculous and they expect it. To label this expectation as ignorance and superstition is a very simple solution, and like most simple solutions, it is an arbitrary dismissal of a problem.

If the naturalist says that it is impossible to see how natural man could distinguish the preternatural in a natural setting, one can give an easy answer. If the numinous wishes to be made known in history, he could also aid the powers of human knowledge with his aid. Grace could make me distinguish even though we were to admit that without it the recognition of the miraculous would not be forthcoming. If the naturalist objects that this introduces a disorderly factor into scientific investigation we can only answer that the disorder is present only because the order erected was produced arbitrarily. The naturalist is at heart a determinist. In a free universe, freely created and freely directed, there is no difficulty in admitting different types of action. The question is whether the world is a texture of iron determinism in terms of nature or texture of freedom where nature and God operate, and God operates with fullest freedom tolerating no restrictions from nature. That God determines all things must be admitted, but such determination denies neither his freedom nor the freedom of human agents.

What is more, given a perfectly balanced observer with his intelligence acute, he would be able to distinguish between the natural and the supernatural, for the natural bears its own distinguishing marks on its being and so does the supernatural. It can readily be admitted that this perfectly balanced thinker is not to be found on this earth as we know it, but the difficulty in distinguishing the supernatural derives not from intelligence as such, but from unbalance. That such unbalance, called Original Sin in theological terminology, requires God to give the human observer a grace, at least sanative, we can easily concede.

The recognition of a divine break-through into history is not the same as the reception of a divine communication that requires no construction on the part of the recipient. Here we have a different form of knowledge, though it is generically an assent to testimony. The divine message must be achieved divinely, i.e., in the meaning that God attaches to the message and with the divine command stamped all over it. The recognition that God broke into history is not enough to make such an assent. The whole knowing apparatus must be energized divinely in order to grasp the message not on the natural order but on the divine.

This kind of knowledge clearly does not fall into the field of philosophic epistemology which according to its method does not deal with the supernatural as such. But on the other hand, philosophic epistemology must not rule out such knowledge.

Seventh, mysticism throws a revealing light on knowledge. It supposes that the mind is at core intuitive, not only of the phenomenal self and the meanings of phenomenal objects, but of something beyond the self and meaning. Mysticism shows that the very heart of reality can be grasped immediately. That this is supernatural in the present order of things we can cheerfully admit, but natural or supernatural, the mind is shown to have vast capacities which far exceed the abstractive process normal to our daily experience. More than this: even abstraction will only be an inferior manifestation of the great power of the spirit. Knowledge is not only intuitive in its roots but also in its flower.

Such we submit are the epistemological commitments arising from the presence of the numinous in knowledge. Let it not be objected that we have not proved the objectivity of the numinous. Epistemology cannot deal with that question. It can only deal with knowledge and it is not free to exclude any object from its knowledge area, if the object is not logically contradictory. Given a peculiar object as antecedently not impossible, epistemology must be constructed so that this object can be known consistently with all other objects. The religious object shakes all epistemological schemes to the ground if they do not wish to deal with it, and it will give a peculiar scheme to epistemology if the object is permitted to play its part.

Part II

Can philosophy provide
a rational justification
of man's religious activity?

6

The Problem

What Can Metaphysics Dictate to Man in the Field of Religion?

In the first part of this study we have seen that of the various answers to the question: how can the human mind know the numinous? one of the positive metaphysical answers was that man can intellectually justify the knowledge of the numinous by a reasoned reflection on reality.[1] In this part we shall make a further study of this philosophical approach to the knowledge of God. It is not our intention to set down a systematic natural theology, nor yet a revealed theology, but rather a meditation on the notion of theology itself and hence of its presuppositions. One way of putting it would be to say that this part of our study deals with the three blank pages that lead to the title page of a theology textbook. We can never deal with any subject without supposing many things. If we ask, how can we know God?, we are supposing that we can know God and we are supposing a determined notion of God. Any good text of natural theology presents a coherent doctrine concerning God and easily refutes all objections to its findings by referring to postulates which are or are not stated. It is impossible to state all the postulates with which an investigator begins, yet these postulates are the dynamism of his discoveries and conclusions. Susanne Langer aptly quotes A. N. Whitehead:

> When you are criticising the philosophy of an epoch, do not chiefly direct your attention to those intellectual positions which its exponents feel it necessary explicitly to defend. There will be some fundamental assumptions which adherents of all the variant systems within the epoch unconsciously presuppose. Such assumptions appear so obvious that people do not know what they are assuming because no other way of putting things has ever occurred to them. With these assumptions a certain number of types of

---

[1] Cf. Chapter 2, "Rational verification of the numinous."

95

philosophic systems are possible, and this group of systems constitutes the
philosophy of the epoch.[2]

Consequently, we now wish to investigate the postulates of natural
theology or theodicy,[3] to use the Leibnizian term for it, in the light of
the findings of our own investigations into metaphysics, epistemology,
and religion. At the outset let us summarize our own notions concerning
metaphysics, epistemology, and religion.

*We equate philosophy and metaphysics, and define philosophy as the
thought-discipline which proceeds from the real considered in terms of
meanings, achieved spontaneously by the mind in its search of the real,
to the rational erection of a hierarchic system of principles derived from
the meanings, in order to give the ultimate understanding of reality in
as far as it is assimilable by the natural human mind.*

*By epistemology we understand an analytic reflection on human knowl-
edge in order to recognize its inevitable commitments, its limits, and its
vulnerability to error.*

*In the light of epistemology, disciplined methods can be constructed
in order to avoid error in definite fields of investigation. Two outstanding
methods of this kind are philosophy and science, which are two distinct
though complementary methods.*

*We have seen in the first part of this work that by religion we mean
human behavior in as far as it is directed toward an object called God.
By God we mean roughly what Rudolf Otto has called the "numinous,"
an object, accepted as real, on which the human subject is totally dependent; which object is totally other and beyond our categories; which is,
in consequence, involved in frightening obscurity, a* mysterium tremendum, *a fascinating, majestic superiority.*[4]

Having indicated what we mean by the words we use, let us clearly
indicate the problem that we wish to investigate. The question that we

---

[2] Susanne K. Langer, *Philosophy in a New Key*, (Cambridge, Mass., Harvard University Press, 1951), pp. 4-5. Quoted with permission of the Harvard University Press.
Permission to include the passage from Whitehead has been granted by The Macmillan Company, publishers of A. N. Whitehead, *Science and the Modern World*.
The quotation appears in Chapter 3 of that work.

[3] The term "theodicy" is generally used, and is here used, to mean the proofs for
the existence of God. It sometimes has a more restricted meaning of the vindication
of the justice and providence of God in view of the presence of evil in the world.

[4] The notion of religion has been adequately dealt with in Part I of this study.
The notions of epistemology and metaphysics have been more fully treated in another
work, Gustave Weigel and Arthur G. Madden, *Knowledge: Its Values and Limits*
(Englewood Cliffs, N.J.: Prentice-Hall, Inc., 1961), which gives a general theory of
knowledge and a critique of the method of science and that of metaphysics.

propose for ourselves is this: What can metaphysics (philosophy) dictate to man in the field of religion?

A priori, certain answers are possible:

(1) Metaphysics can rationally justify the religious enterprise, without delimiting it precisely.
(2) Metaphysics can deduce an adequate religious scheme.
(3) Metaphysics refutes the religious claims.
(4) Metaphysics has nothing to say about religion at all.

No two of these propositions can be maintained simultaneously. Perhaps other answers are possible, but certainly the four proposed are clear, intelligible answers.

7

History of the Problem

It is obvious that our problem is not new. It has been with us for a long time. In philosophy it is the question of natural theology as it has been called since the time of Christian Wolff (1679-1754). Kant has said somewhere: "It is absolutely necessary to be convinced of the existence of God; but it is not so necessary to prove it." Without wishing to ask the question how one can be convinced without proof of some kind or other, we can say that Kant's dictum expresses the thought of great numbers of men of all times. The fact seems to be that philosophy raised the doubt as to the existence of the divine, thus attacking religion at its very heart. Plato says well:

> For if the foregoing statements [against the existence of the gods] had not been disseminated among practically all men, it would not be necessary to present reasons for the existence of the gods. But now there is need to do so.[1]

Plato was perhaps the first who offered a theodicy in an extended form, and it can be found in his tenth book of the *Laws*. He proposes three arguments for the existence of the divine or gods: (1) The phenomenon of design in nature (2) The universal consent of all races in the belief in the divine (3) All being must be reduced to a psychic force.[2]

The difficulty with Plato is that his reduction of reality to psyche leaves us in doubt if he believed that the divine was truly personal. Yet it is true that he believes in a foreknowing and provident God. Although he rejects the mythical accounts of the gods as falsifying the nature of the

---

[1] *Laws*, Book X, 891b.
[2] Cf. Paul Elmer More, *The Religion of Plato* (Princeton, N.J.: Princeton University Press, 1928).

divine,[3] yet he does not clearly explain anywhere his own conception of the divinity. The word *theos*, singular or plural, is always obscure in Greek literature.

Aristotle

Aristotle seems to have had less religion than his master. Yet he was preoccupied with the problem of God, and for him, as for Plato, it was the first philosophic question. Hence he deals with the notion in his First Philosophy, called today *Metaphysics*. This discipline, as distin-guished from cosmology and mathematics, he calls "theology,"[4] because it deals with the divine, the "immovable substance."

In the twelfth book of the *Metaphysics* we have the natural theology of Aristotle.[5] The conclusions of Aristotle are interesting, not so much for what he may have understood by them, as for the start they gave Saint Thomas, and through him all the post-Thomistic thinkers. We present the Aristotelian propositions:

> Indeed, life too belongs to God; for the actuality of mind is life and he is that actuality; and his absolute actuality is life most excellent and eternal. We affirm then that God is living, eternal, most excellent, so that life and an unintermittent and eternal duration belong to God; for this is the very reality of God.[6]

> It is evident, therefore, from what has been said, that there is a substance, eternal and unmoved and existing apart from the objects of the senses. Likewise has it been demonstrated that it is impossible for this substance to have magnitude; rather it is without parts and is indivisible (for it puts things in motion through limitless time, for nothing that is limited has un-limited power; and since every magnitude is unlimited or limited, it would not for the reason just mentioned have limited magnitude. Nor could it have unlimited magnitude because an unlimited magnitude is quite impossible). Yet it has also been demonstrated that it is impassive and unchangeable; for all the other changes are subsequent to change of place.[7]

Now it is wise to see how Aristotle got to these propositions. The whole twelfth book deals with the motion of the heavenly bodies and from this motion Aristotle derives his unmovable mover, who moves

---

[3] Plato, *Laws*, X, 886.
[4] Aristotle, *Metaphysics*, VI, 1026a.
[5] *Ibid.*, 1071b-1073b.
[6] *Ibid.*, XII, 1072b.
[7] *Ibid.*, XII, 1073a.

as a final cause. The Aristotelian spheres must be moved and so he puts a motor beyond the spheres, and thus beyond space and consequently beyond spatial limitations. Its activity consists in its non-spatial goodness, or life in thought, which attracts the first sphere to act, and its first motion must be spheric.

Now whatever be the value of the metaphysical principles involved in Aristotle's reasoning, the use of them on a cosmos of spheres and the postulate that all movement of a spatial entity is primarily spatial and in a circle, plus the doctrine that the forty-seven spheres are divinities knowing the prime divinity and, by love of it, in action,[8] must make a modern man pause as to the legitimacy of the Aristotelian conclusions.

The Aristotelian God is a *deus ex machina* and a borrowing of the religious content of the myths which were the basis of Greek literature.[9] Aristotle cannot have a concentric system of spheres in motion without something outside of the spheres accounting for their motion, and since this reality is outside of space, he must give it the non-spatial reality of thought which is life. This God has no efficient influence on the cosmos, no concern for it, no part in its production, and no joy and no sadness deriving from the fate of the cosmos. The world goes its way because of inner drives, and God goes on contemplating himself. God's presence makes the thinking spheres, or gods, love him, and because of this love they are set in motion. Whatever be the reality of God, for Aristotle he is only a device whereby his system of spheres can move. This device he gladly accepted because he found that the ancient myths, which everyone knew and which commanded sentimental adhesion at least, prepared the mind for the acceptance of the device. It is useless to pray to Aristotle's God, nor did Aristotle expect anybody to pray to him. Much less did it occur to Aristotle that we should do God's will, because God had no will with regard to us. Aristotle's God is not a religious object but only a philosophical hypothesis. To sell this hypothesis he makes an appeal to religion, but he does not justify religion by his hypothesis.

The theodicies of Plato and Aristotle are the first attempts at rational defense of the existence of God. Both men proceed homogeneously with their basic visions. Aristotle joins a natural theology to his theodicy. Plato gives his theodicy in the *Laws* but his divine cosmogony in the *Timaeus*.[10] Plato uses myth as the vehicle of communication while Aristotle avoids the myth and speaks in accord with logic. The myth-technique of Plato, leaving the obscure though faintly glimpsed, lends

---

[8] *Ibid.*, XII, 1074a and b.

[9] *Ibid.*, XII, 1074b.

[10] *Timaeus*, 27d-69a.

itself to understanding on other frameworks of thought. It is a pregnant expression. Aristotle gives us seemingly precise reasoning which lends itself to any approach to the God-problem.

However, when all is said and done, the God of Plato need be no god at all. He is the highest Idea, the Good. The Idea is not merely static in the mind of Plato. It is also dynamic. The good as dynamic in the universe Plato calls divine and this divinity has grades as well as other forms of being. Hence Plato can speak of the divine either as the summit of divinity—our God—or as subordinate participations of it, to be called gods or daimons. The intensely personal Yahweh of the Hebrews is not portrayed by the Platonic myth. One might say that Plato would consider Yahweh most ungodlike. Plato's God is an ideal reality active as an ideal is active. By reason of his rhetorical use of the myth, this ideal reality can be presented as personal, but Plato would not wish us to take such expressions too literally, though he himself would not know where to draw the line. If a synthesis of his thought could be essayed without too much temerity, we might say that for Plato the real is nuclearly ideal, with the highest ideal at its center. The ideal is dynamic in a universe where, beside the ideal, the material is equally present, receiving the influence of the ideal as dynamically directive. Plato can be understood pantheistically, monotheistically, polytheistically, and—strangely enough —atheistically. As a matter of fact he has been understood in all these senses. Religion is possible in Plato because of the imprecision of the mythological mode of expression.

Aristotle's God, as we have seen, is a physical and not ideal entity, the final bond that keeps the solid universe together, preventing it from dissolving itself in space. It is a thought, rendered functional in the Aristotelian system by the trick of making thought thinking and thus actual. Religion is meaningless in Aristotle, except as a recognition of the realities of the universe. Surrender to God is a concept that is meaningless to Aristotle. In its place he would substitute acceptance of the universe.

The Epicureans

As Plato said, atheism was rampant in the fourth century B.C. of Greek culture. In addition to Sophists and Cynics, the man who gave it wings was Democritus with his idea of a universe which grows out of chance. This view was taken over by Epicurus. In *De Rerum Natura,* Lucretius has given us the noblest expression of this philosophy. As

Lucretius sees it, it is the task of the philosopher to rid men of the fear of the gods. Religion is for him evil.

> For such great evils could religion solicit men! [11]

> Thus, to be sure, does dread constrain all men because they see many things happen on earth and in the sky, the causes of which they can by no means observe, and so conclude that they are brought about by a divinity. For these reasons, when we shall have realized that nothing can be produced from nothing, we shall then have a more accurate insight into the objects of our investigation, namely, whence each thing can be produced and how each can come to be without the agency of the gods.[12]

> The rest of the phenomena which mortals see happening on earth and in the sky, when, as often, they hang in uncertainty with fearful thoughts, also lower their courage and crush them to earth with dread of the gods, because ignorance of causes impels them to consign all things to the rule of the gods and to yield dominion to them. For if those who have rightly learned that the gods live a life that is free of cares, nevertheless wonder in the meantime what plan there is in accordance with which each thing is brought to pass, especially those things which are observed in the regions of the sky, these wretched people are landing right back in their old worship of the gods, adopting harsh masters whom they suppose to be omnipotent. They are ignorant of what is possible and impossible, and finally why a determinate power and deep-seated limit is given to each thing. The result is that they are led all the more into error by blind reasoning. If you do not reject from your mind such thoughts, and cease entertaining beliefs unworthy of the gods and in contradiction to their peaceful existence, the holy powers of the gods, belittled by you, will often oppose you. Not that the supreme power of the gods could really be so dishonored that out of wrath they would determine to exact harsh punishment, but because you will imagine that the gods, who safely dwell in serene and quiet peace, churn with great waves of wrath, you will not visit the shrines of the gods with a quiet heart, nor will you be able with peace of mind to receive those images which are carried from their sacred bodies into the minds of men as signs of their divine perfection.[13]

Lucretius is only the Latin expositor of Epicurus who erected the physical theories of Democritus into a transcendental philosophy called Epicureanism. This philosophy, strangely enough, did not deny the gods. It merely made them useless in the framework of the universe. They lived in a place apart, happy, carefree, and without passion. Their passionless existence made them models for men, and thus they were

---

[11] *De Rerum Natura*, I, 100.

[12] *Ibid.*, I, 151-158.

[13] *Ibid.*, VI, 50-78.

religiously useful in the sense that they stimulated man to overcome passions in order to achieve peace. However, the gods had no influence on the world and men, and they were products of the universal forces no less than all other things.

It is a wonder that the Epicureans accepted the gods at all. Their philosophy does not need them. No man had ever seen them. There was no known place for them. Yet Epicurus and Lucretius admitted that they were there. It is easy to say that Epicurus and Lucretius tried to avoid shocking their contemporaries with an out and out atheism, quite contrary to the classical prejudices. However, this solution does not seem adequate. The gods are conspicuous in Epicurean philosophy. They have a function, but the function is pedagogic. Epicurus wishes to produce a tranquil soul, accepting a universe which moves inexorably and reducing desire to a non-disturbing minimum. Examples of such behavior are the gods. Religion thus has a place in his thought, but it must be a reformed religion. The gods remind us to be restrained and at peace. Thus religion is not cult or obeisance to the gods, nor a wish-fulfilling device but a symbolic moral teaching.

Epicurus and Lucretius do not prove that the gods exist. They merely frame their philosophy to make room for them. This was gladly done, because Epicurus wanted *real* exemplars of the goal he set up for men. Their belief in the gods could serve him in his ethical enterprise.

The Stoics

After Aristotle two philosophies competed for the mind of the Hellenic world—the Epicureans and the Stoics. As we have seen, the gods of the Epicureans were useless to men, as Marcus Aurelius the Stoic saw:

> Now if the gods take no concern about anything—this is impious to believe, or else let us not sacrifice nor pray to them, nor swear by them, nor do any of the other things which we are accustomed to direct to the gods, as though they are present and dwelling among us! [14]

The Stoics, however, were close to the divine. The writings of Epictetus and Marcus Aurelius exude piety. Yet in neither writer do we find a developed natural theology. It seems that their theology could be summarized as follows: the universe is one whole, formed of matter and spirit, which spirit, reductively material, is the world-soul, shared by

---

[14] *Meditations*, VI, 44.

individual men because they reason and think. Using the Platonic principle of the reduction of all reality to psyche, the real is reduced to the world-psyche which is called God, the gods, the divine, Zeus. He is the creator in the sense that he orders the universe by a providence which is total. Using the Aristotelian concept of the spheres, they conceived the spheres as divine and gods, subject to the supreme deity, called Zeus or God. Wisdom for the Stoics consisted in accepting the will of the gods with contentment, realizing that this will, governing all things, is to the benefit of all. The deity is so close to us that we are truly children of God and therefore all brothers and citizens of the world with God as king.

Although Epictetus and Marcus Aurelius do not propose a theodicy, they were both aware of its need. Epictetus outlines the program of a theodicy,[15] but he does not carry out the project. Scattered through his writings we find the following arguments for the existence of God. God is the necessary cause of all things;[16] the universe is one and God is the root of unity;[17] the design or fittingness of all things indicates the work of an artificer and not mere chance.[18] In two places Marcus Aurelius proposes a theodicy. It is difficult even to conceive of the gods not taking forethought for the good of each man, or at least of the universe as a whole. What motive could impel them to do me evil?[19] Again, the invisibility of the gods refers only to the senses; they are perceptible in their works.[20]

As can be seen by this rapid glance at Hellenic philosophy from Plato to Marcus Aurelius, no system defended atheism. The Epicureans had a system where the gods were seemingly superfluous, but the system none the less preserved a conspicuous place for the gods. The gods of Epicurus and of Aristotle were not true religious objects, because they did not determine anything about man. The divinity of Plato and of the Stoics was a true religious object, yet the nature of this divinity expressed in their philosophy is most obscure, and though they speak of the divine as personal, still it is not clear that the Platonic or Stoic divinities were more than reason at work in the universe. All the philosophies took it for granted that religion would be practiced in accord with the mores of their peoples. They consider this good, but they do not philosophize about it.

---

[15] *Discourses*, I, xii.
[16] *Ibid.*, I, xvi.
[17] *Ibid.*, I, xiv.
[18] *Ibid.*, I, vi; I, xvi.
[19] *Meditations*, VI, 44.
[20] *Ibid.*, XII, 28.

The Hebrew-Christian Impact

While Plato and Aristotle were theorizing, one people of classical times had as a national heritage a vital awareness of God as absolute lord, intensely personal, utterly invisible, unique, and the sole Deity. This people, Israel, was isolationist with a greater contempt for the non-Jew than the Hellenes had for the "barbarians." Israel was chauvinistically isolationist, yet the conquering imperialisms of the times crushed the Jews and scattered them over the Mediterranean world. The polytheism, pantheism, and moral laxity of the Greek world shocked the Jew. His own religious tradition as expressed in the Hebrew scriptures gave no philosophic support to Jewish religion, nor did it essay a theodicy. It is true that the book of *Job* makes some philosophic reflections on the governance of the world by God, but there is no systematic treatment of the theme. The Book of the Preacher, or *Ecclesiastes,* attributed to Solomon, sounds rather Epicurean in its approach to the question of life and God. On the other hand, Jewish mores were more congenial to Stoic high-mindedness, and according to Moses Hadas[21] there was a Jewish influence in the creation of Stoicism.

In spite of the congeniality of Stoicism, the Jewish tradition was not philosophical. The philosophical drive of the Hellenic world would inevitably affect some Jews and draw them into that form of investigation. The best of such work was done by Philo of Alexandria (c.20 B.C.-40 A.D.) who found Plato's piety acceptable to the Jewish spirit and made Plato hebraically orthodox by the simple process of reversing the Platonic vision. For Plato, God is the supreme Idea; but Philo twisted this to make all the Ideas thoughts of God who was the creator by producing out of nothing, a notion dismayingly novel to the Hellenic tradition. Two centuries later the Christian writers, Clement (d.216) and Origen (185-254), from Philo's city, Alexandria, would follow the road of Philo and rework Platonism to make it a Christian vision of divinity. But the first Christians were not interested in theodicy, though Paul, in his Epistle to the Romans,[22] had given a brief theodicy that is identical with that later given by Marcus Aurelius. How Platonic it is, is difficult to say.

It is worth our while to study the Pauline theodicy, because it is the

---

[21] Moses Hadas, "Shem in the Tents of Japeth," chap. iv of *Science, Philosophy and Religion, A Symposium* (New York: Conference on Science, Philosophy and Religion, 1941).

[22] *Romans* I, 18-32.

first Christian attempt at this kind of work. The Pauline statement is very brief and quite cryptic. He says that God revealed himself to the philosophers of Hellenism, because even though invisible, his visible works manifest his power and divinity. No more is said, and a rhetorical contrast is developed. The philosophers corrupted the figure of God by portraying him as a man or beast, and God in revenge corrupts the human being by reducing him below the animal plane, manifested in the unnatural vices of the Hellenic world.

In Marcus Aurelius the argument, so like that of Saint Paul, quite probably means that the philosopher by introspection finds God working in his own soul. In Saint Paul it seems to refer to God's external creation, and so we have something like the argument called cosmological in Kantian language. God is the efficient cause of the universe, and its beauty and rationality manifest the power and divinity of the creator. Yet the Pauline argument is not the simple appeal to the cause of the universe, which is a static argument. For Paul, God reveals himself in his creation, that is, the purpose of the creation is to speak to men so that the world is God's word whereby he speaks to human beings. There is a personal relationship of communication between God and men in creation itself. It is to the point to indicate that Paul does not define God, but supposes that his readers have had a personal realization of what and who he is. Even the pagans according to Paul heard and understood God's word. It was something more vital than a mere syllogism.

This teaching of Saint Paul is very illuminating. In him two different drives meet to form a new theodicetic approach to God. Paul, true to his Israelitic training, lives close to God. This God is not the aloof, unminding God of Aristotle, or the distant, blissful beings of the Epicureans. Paul's God is the God of Israel who commands men, punishes them, rewards, coaxes, and loves them. Epictetus could speak of God as the father of men, and men the children of God, but only Israel could see in God the jealous spouse of a fickle bride called Israel. The Israelite does not search for God; Yahweh searches out Abraham, Isaac, and Jacob. The Israelite does not use his energies to discover God; God *reveals himself* to the people. The task of the Jew was not to construct a worldview and a God-concept. He was to accept the God who reveals himself with no theorizing about it at all. This is the religion of the Hebrew books. God reveals himself as the creator; the Jew does not reason from the world to God. Consequently when Saint Paul uses the Hellenic argument of cosmic causality, he gives it a Jewish twist. It is not the simple Hellenic reflection that the cosmos must have a source, which is metaphysical reasoning, but rather an extension of the Hebraic notion of the revealing God. To Israel God revealed himself by speaking to the patriarchs in theophanies and to the people at large through his prophets who were the spokesmen of God, and for Paul the greatest and last of these prophets is Jesus Christ the Lord. To the gentiles God also spoke, but not in the familiar fashion as he did with Israel. There was a vaguer theophany which had to suffice for the gentiles, but it was a theophany— a self-revealing of God. In his creative works God revealed himself to the gentiles. Just as with Israel, the gentile was not called upon to construct his God. God came to him and the gentile heard his voice in the winds which swept over the city and the land, and the wind showed Yahweh's power and absolute lordship. In Saint Paul the purely rational reflection of Aristotle or Epictetus takes on personal dimensions. It is not merely reasoned discourse; it is essentially a personal dialogue. That is why the gentiles were without excuse, for they heard Yahweh and *knew* him, and not merely understood a theory about him.

This Pauline theodicy is something startlingly new in the Hellenic thought-world. Plato deprecates the myths of Attica as unworthy of the divinity, because Plato has by reason and insight constructed his God. Aristotle finds in the myths a grain of truth, but because of his cosmology he must cut away from the myths all that will not fit his construct. Epicurus is so concentrated on man, that the gods for him are only patterns which man can use fruitfully. Epictetus finds God within himself, because thought is divine. Paul hears God outside of himself, and God must be accepted as any reality in experience. Paul makes no construction. This idea upset the whole Greek way of thinking about God.

Neo-Platonism

The Jewish and Christian impact on classical thought produced a change in classical thinking. The man who manifests this change without becoming Christian is Plotinus (c.204-c.270). By the third century it was clear to all that Hellenic religion was unsatisfactory. Society still kept the temples of Jupiter and Venus, because this cult was traditional; however, the people were looking for salvation and tried the different eastern cults which absorbed the worshipper into the divinity. Aristotle's God was religiously unsatisfactory and in consequence Plato, who was pious, was studied again. The Jews and the Christians had a pure God and a personal God. The superiority of this God was stressed by all the Christian apologetes. Plotinus, clinging to Plato, found in Platonic piety pointers to a personal God. According to Paul Henry, S.J., there can be no doubt that Plotinus believed in a God more personal than in Plato, at least in the sense that he was a living consciousness exercising love.[23] According to Henry, Plotinus is not a formal pantheist, but a virtual one, because he teaches the necessary emanation of all things from the One. In other words, Plotinism logically involves pantheism.

Plotinus certainly had a high concept of God. He was also interested in piety, and piety must lead to the mystical experience or pure intuition of the reality of the One. Plotinus shows us that the classical world of the late second and total third centuries was living in an environment of God-consciousness, because it never occurs to Plotinus to give a theodicy but only a theology. The widespread tendency to atheism of which Plato complains in the tenth book of the *Laws* seems to have disappeared. Yet Epictetus makes it clear that in his time, c. A.D. 50-c. 125, there were atheists, nor does he consider them rarities. It is safe to say that the atheists were merely unorganized sceptics, flourishing from the fourth century B.C. to the second century A.D. Certainly no systematic philosophy of wide appeal taught or defended atheism. Stoics and Epicureans were materialists but they were not atheists. The Epicureans admitted no divine direction of events nor the existence of divine laws, but they yet accepted the gods. The non-importance of atheism in the third century A.D. is obvious from Plotinus' total neglect of any theodicetic endeavors. That God was, was taken for granted by Plotinus, and probably by his entire age.

The Fathers

The Christian thinkers now called the Fathers are the philosophers of the fourth and fifth centuries, who accept Christianity as the matrix of their thinking. Those who were interested in theory borrowed Platonic frameworks for construction. Origen is the first great constructor, though his road was prepared by Clement. Basil and the Cappadocians follow the lead of Origen, the Master. In the West the great figure is Augustine, who not only follows Plato, but is influenced by Neo-Platonism. None of these men is interested in theodicy, though obviously they are theologians. In this period the doctrine of the triune God is hammered out amid blood and sweat. The divinity of Christ is being accurately formulated, and in the fifth century it will take on the form of hypostatic union to the rejection of moral union or the fusion of two natures in one.

---

[23] Cf. *Enneads*, 5,4,2; 5,1,6; 6,8,13 ff.

Echoes of Platonic and Aristotelian theodicy can be found in these thinkers.[24] The design which Plato thought he saw in the universe is often stressed. The cosmological argument, i.e., God is the first cause of all, shows up here and there. However, in no Father do we find any anxiety for theodicy. The typically Jewish-Christian doctrine of the knowledge of God through personal encounter is absolutely predominant. The role of Christ and the Church in this encounter is being analyzed and formulated, but there is no theodicy involved in the enterprise.

Anselm of Canterbury

The fifth century brought with it the collapse of the Western Roman Empire and also inaugurated the isolation and inbreeding of the Byzantine world. The Western collapse, produced by the invasion of the Germanic tribes possessing a simpler and ruder culture than that of the peoples whom they overcame, was not a final thing. The collapse only demanded the task of reconstructing the new mass into a new form. Only the Church with the Roman Bishop at its head was capable of such an enterprise. The Roman Church guided the total Western Church, and the Church produced a legal and intellectual framework for social living. The result was Western Christendom, a political confederation of peoples accepting as primary the Roman Catholic religion under the guidance of the Bishop of Rome. Boniface VIII in the fourteenth century was not wrong when he appealed to the constitution of Western Christendom, declaring it to be the civil arrangement of Catholic life, so that civil rulers were only the Church's vicars in matters temporal, subject to the final dictamen of the Church, and therefore the Pope. This civic arrangement changed with the rise of nationalism at the end of the thirteenth century.

After the collapse of the Roman arrangement in the fifth century, the task of reconstruction was slow. Unassimilated Germanic tribes were on the prowl for two centuries more and the Moslems in Spain were at Europe's western door, after having taken Northern Africa out of the sphere of Roman Catholicism. From the sixth to the eighth century the task was the conservation of order by adapting and modifying old Roman procedures to the new mind and the new people. The scholar and the saint, in order to have the tranquility his work demanded, retired to the mountains and the islands. The monk's isolation did not give him

---

[24] Cf. Augustine's *De Trinitate*.

the stimulus of actual life in his meditations; he pored over the writings of the past, and in that atmosphere of thought he stayed. In the ninth century the Franks organized a large area of Europe into a fairly stable cultural pattern, and in the shadow of the Frankish chieftains, especially Charlemagne (742-814), the intellectual could ply his trade in isolation and in peace. The Charlemagnian patronage in favor of schools gave birth to a new way of thinking, a way that has subsequently been called Scholasticism, because it was the way of the schools rather than of the past or of the monasteries. In the beginning, men like Alcuin (c.730-804) could only communicate to a new people the learning of the past which had been conserved in the monasteries, especially in the isolated and therefore protected Celtic centers of the northern isles. However, the meeting of ancient thought with a new environment produced gradually a new thought.

The new environment needed no theodicy, because social life was grounded on Catholicism, which was a religious configuration wherein the reality of God was just taken for granted, and the meaning of God defined by the formulas of the ancient councils and divines. The classical writers were spontaneously understood in a Catholic sense, even though the classical thought was quite distinct from the new understanding. Hence Scotus Erigena (c.810-877), the first bright light of the new thought, uses the Platonism he inherited from the Fathers by way of the monasteries, and with it explains the real as he knew it, which meant in the first place the Catholic scheme of things. The pantheism of Platonism did not harmonize well with the personal God of the Catholics, and this was soon seen by the contemporaries and successors of Erigena. In the ninth and tenth centuries the Catholic thinkers were still in search of a philosophic framework adequate for the synthesis of knowledge based on the Catholic faith. They groped and they experimented in fragmentary fashion.

One factor of the time put the Catholics on the defensive. In southern Spain with Cordoba as the center, the Moslems had peace, prosperity, and distance from the narrowly conservative Mohammedan mentality of the Middle East. The result was a non-Catholic intellectual ferment from the tenth century on. The Arabs discovered Aristotle and used him rather than Plato as their dialectical framework. The Arabs also engaged successfully in mathematics, astronomy, and medicine, and their work penetrated into Catholic Europe, especially through Sicily and southern Italy. This was non-Catholic thought and the Catholics were against it, but they were affected by it.

Needless to say, the thorough impregnation of Western European society by Catholicism as the nucleus of social reality channeled medieval thought into theology above all else. Theology, however, needs some philosophy, and so philosophy was indirectly cultivated.

Any discipline, which in history is initially formed without too much theoretical reflection, will finally raise the question: why this way? The first European who seems to have felt this question was Anselm of Canterbury (1033-1109). He was born in Aosta near Turin in northern Italy, went to the famous monastery of Bec in Normandy where in 1078 he succeeded Lanfranc as Abbot, and succeeded the same Lanfranc as Archbishop of Canterbury in 1093. He took conspicuous part in the eleventh century Council of Bari in southern Italy, to arrange the reunion of the Byzantine Catholics of Sicily and Italy. He was a well-traveled man of learning and deep spirituality. He was canonized by the Church.

Anselm is well aware of the question: why theology? He was also aware of the Arabs in Spain. This double awareness produced two interesting little books, the *Monologium* and *Proslogium*.[25]

These two little works, along with the response to the monk of Marmoutier, Gaunilo, who attacked the reasoning of the *Proslogium,* are all fruits of the monastery days of Anselm. The little tomes manifest first of all a man of piety, humility, meditation, high intelligence, and a thorough knowledge of Saint Augustine. The *Monologium* is the first developed theodicy in the history of mankind. We have seen that Plato and Aristotle constructed theodicies, but these fitted into greater works as parts. Anselm writes an independent and complete theodicy. It need surprise no one that all subsequent theodicies of a rational type rely on him directly or indirectly.

Most people think of Anselm as the author of the so-called ontological argument and as nothing else. That argument he does not propose in the *Monologium* but in its successor the *Proslogium*. In the *Monologium* we have a variety of arguments given, which will later be taken up by Saint Thomas in the Five Ways. In the first chapter Anselm shows that the Platonic preoccupation with the good necessarily points to the supreme good. The argument is totally Platonic. Good is such of itself or by participation. If it is good of itself, then it is singular. If it is plural, it is good by participation in goodness, and so goodness is supposed as prior to the good things. Thus, there can be no plurality of the goods unless they participate in the goodness of the first supreme good.

---

[25] Anselm's works can be found in the *Patrologia Latina* (ed. Migne), Vols. 158 and 159. All of Anselm's works here mentioned are in Vol. 158.

This same argument is then repeated by substituting existence for goodness.[26] Everything that exists, exists by participation or of itself. That which exists of itself must be singular, for otherwise the many supposed *per se* existents would share a common existence, and thus be participated existence. In this proof the notion of cause is in play, and also the difference between essence and existence, which distinction Anselm clearly recognizes.[27] Therefore his proof includes the argument of act and potency though it is not put in an Aristotelian way. The argument explicitly includes the argument from the degrees of being.[28]

In other words, of the Five Ways of Saint Thomas, Anselm gives three. He argues from cause, from the priority of existence to potency, and from the degrees of being. Anselm does not give the Aristotelian argument of the Prime Immovable Motor, nor does he give the argument from design. That he should ignore the Aristotelian argument is not surprising, because he derives all his thinking from Platonism. Why did he omit the argument from design which is Platonic, and which is in Saint Augustine whom Anselm follows? We think the reason is obvious by reason of the type of thinking involved in the *Monologium*. The appeal is exclusively metaphysical, and no physical proof is considered, or even in place.

In the *Monologium* Anselm also gives us the derivation of the Trinity from the concept of God the creator. He takes the Pauline notion we have already seen, namely, that creation is a divine *locutio,* God's speaking.[29] Yet he is led to this not by the Pauline notion of God's revealing himself to man, but because in God there is a Logos, a Word. Hence Anselm's notion of creation as a speaking is Johannine and Platonic, not Pauline.[30]

In this conception of creation as a speaking, as a self-expression, Anselm introduces the whole Platonic world of Ideas, but Anselm follows Augustine by understanding the Ideas as conceptual objects of the divine mind.[31] Anselm's theodicy also contains the derivation of divine attributes other than the Trinity. God is substantial, immutable, eternal, omnipresent, spiritual.

Now if from this description of the *Monologium,* one were to suppose that Anselm is a simple Platonic rationalist, a grievous error would be made. Anselm insists on a real creation against emanationism—it is

---

[26] *Monologium,* chapters 3-8.
[27] Cf. last paragraph of c.7.
[28] Cf. first paragraph of c.4.
[29] Cf. c.10; c.34; c.35; c.36.
[30] Cf. c.35.
[31] Cc.9-11.

creatio ex nihilo sui.[32] He insists that the doctrine of the Trinity is mysterious, that it cannot be gained by pure reason, but must be believed.[33] In fact, Anselm sees the need of dealing with the question of faith and its applicability to this whole problem.[34]

Our modern semanticists should be happy with Anselm, too. He appreciates the semantic problems and shows that he knows them, and he tries to resolve them by an analysis of meaning. He will even meet the Barthians who stress the ineffability of God, for Anselm recognizes that words are used analogously and imperfectly when applied to the divinity. Anselm's rationalism is neither naïve nor dogmatic nor extreme.

Great as was the contribution of the *Monologium,* that work is overlooked and few realize that all subsequent Christian theodicies derive from it, including the theodicy of Saint Thomas. The reason for this neglect is that a different contribution of Anselm, the ontological argument, has given him notoriety, for with it Anselm's name is always associated. This approach, which perhaps was latent in the *Monologium,* was developed for the first time in a subsequent little work called the *Proslogium,* a real gem of theological and philosophical thinking.

In the preface to the *Proslogium* Anselm tells us that it is a later work than the *Monologium.* He there also tells us that the earlier title of the *Monologium* was "Meditation on the Grounds of Faith", while the name of the second work was "Faith Seeking Understanding." In his final edition of the two works he gave the modern names: *Monologium,* a soliloquy, and *Proslogium,* a discourse.

Now the *Proslogium* does more than give the famous Anselmic argument, which he claims to be original, and it is certainly true that it was never formulated before, though the Platonic reduction of reality to unity and unity to a psychic core is implicitly the same argument. In this little work—only twenty-six short chapters—Anselm stands out, and he stands out as a man of deep piety and great concern for God. The second chapter sounds like a part of the Confessions of Saint Augustine, or a more intellectual chapter of Thomas a Kempis. The little brochure also deals with the attributes of God and with the Trinity. It does not do so with the same detail as the *Monologium,* but it touches all the points. Anselm tells us that he was always looking for an insight into God, whereby the reality of God would overwhelm him immediately. In the *Monologium* he had not achieved his end and therefore he gave in that

---

[32] Cc.7-8. *Creatio ex nihilo sui* means bringing into existence from nothing of himself.

[33] C.38; c.44.

[34] Cc.75-78.

work a number of arguments as we have seen. After having written the *Monologium* he found the immediate argument for the existence of God, and this he now proposes and ties up the rest with it rapidly and succinctly.

Of the entire work the first two chapters are the most important. They define and limit Anselmic rationalism. The first chapter makes it very clear that Anselm starts in faith. He is not trying to justify his faith rationally. He does not doubt at all about the truths of faith, nor does he think that the reader has doubts about faith. Faith for him is a divine gift whereby the obscurity of the intellect corrupted by Original Sin is overcome, and it is the drive of faith which makes us search for understanding. Without faith understanding is impossible. "For I believe this also—that without belief I shall not understand." [35]

What is more the understanding of faith is a divine gift, the result of a revelation. "May I look upwards at your light, whether from far off or from the depths. Teach me to seek you out and show yourself to me in my quest; for neither can I seek you unless you teach me, nor encounter you unless you show yourself." Anselm explicitly rejects the task of reasoning the human intellect into the faith. "For I do not seek to understand in order that I may believe, but I believe in order that I may understand." [36]

It is obvious from these words that Anselm never thought that his argument would be of value to the non-believer. It was the fruit of faith, yet he does say something interesting:

> Thank you, kind Lord, thank you, because that which I previously believed by your gift, I now understand by your enlightening me, so that should I be unwilling to assent to your existence, I would be unable not to understand that you do exist.[37]

The only meaning that we can find in these words is that the argument comes from divine illumination and faith, but once achieved, it is independent of faith, and if faith is lost, the argument still compels. This is an interesting and important position of Anselm.

The Anselmic argument is proposed clearly and simply in the second chapter which deals with the first verse of Psalm 14 (Vulgate, Psalm 13):

---

[35] *Proslogium*, last sentence of chapter I. Karl Barth, *Fides Quaerens Intellectum, Forschungen zur Geschichte und Lehre des Protestantismus*, 4te Reihe, Band. 3 (München: Chr. Kaiser Verlag, 1931), makes much of this initial position of Anselm because it falls in line with the Barthian view of faith and theology.

[36] These citations are also from chapter I.

[37] Last paragraph of chapter IV.

"The fool has said in his heart, there is no God." Anselm puts his argument so:

> And surely that than which a greater cannot be conceived, cannot have being only in the mind. For if it is only in the mind, then it can be conceived to exist also in reality, which is greater.

> If, therefore, that being than which a greater cannot be conceived, has being only in the mind, the very being than which a greater cannot be conceived, is a being than which a greater can be conceived. But surely this cannot be so. Therefore, without doubt there exists a being than which a greater cannot be conceived, and this being is both in the mind and in reality.[38]

Now concerning the value of this argument as conceived by Anselm, we must cling close to Anselm to understand his own evaluation. First of all, the whole scope of the *Proslogium* is to expand the illumination of faith. It is not meant to bring men to the faith. The argument is therefore born in faith and not outside of it. Anselm admits that men can say that God does not exist, even though this involves a contradiction. The reason why such men can say this is because they are foolish.[39] Now this folly is the universal state of man after Original Sin. In the middle of chapter I Anselm laments:

> Whence have we, pitiable ones, been banished; where have we been driven! Whence have we been cast headlong down; where have we been brought to ruin! From our native land into exile, from the sight of God into our own blindness, from joyful immortality to a bitter and dreadful death.

And near the end of the same chapter he says:

> I attest, Lord, and give thanks that you have created in me this likeness of you, that I may be mindful of you, reflect upon you and love you. But it has been so dimmed by the eroding effects of our vices and so obscured by the smoke of our sins, that it cannot attain that for which it was created, unless you renew it and recreate it.

And he winds up the chapter as follows:

> For I believe this also: that without belief I shall not understand.

---

[38] The end of chapter II.
[39] Cf. the end of chapter III.

Consequently, we can say that the fool of whom Anselm speaks in citing
the psalm, is not a demented person or a moron, but rather any man who
is the son of Eve and whose mind has not been recreated by faith. It is,
therefore, not unreasonable to say that for Anselm the ontological argument can be seen only by the believer, though it will retain its force, once
achieved, even though faith disappear. In other words, the understanding
of the argument, which is definitely a rational enterprise, requires a
double predisposing agency; first of all, the state of faith, and secondly,
a further illumination from God, because Anselm had faith long before
he was given the light to see the value of the Anselmic argument and its
formulation. Yet in spite of the necessity of these predispositions, the
argument for Anselm is valid in itself on rational grounds, and therefore,
once achieved, it remains even if faith goes. The argument fulfills perfectly the Anselmic endeavor—faith striving for rational satisfaction, or
at least intellectual satisfaction.

Another insight into the dynamism of the Anselmic argument can be
found in the third chapter at the end of the first paragraph:

> Thus there is indeed some being than which a greater cannot be conceived,
> so that neither can it be conceived to be non-existent. And you are this
> being, O Lord, our God.

It is not straining the thought of Anselm to say that he is thinking on two
lines which finally converge. By meaning-analysis he arrives at the conclusion that there must be a being which by its meaning must exist. By
faith he knows his Lord and God. At this point he pulls the lines together
and the being of metaphysics and the being of God coalesce.

What happens when the thinking is restricted exclusively to the metaphysical line? Does it give God, the object of religion, the numinous reality? It is our opinion that Anselm never gave this question a consideration
In other words, all the subsequent difficulties raised against the Anselmic
argument do not touch Anslem at all, because his adversaries are formu-
lating the argument in a framework he never thought of. For the formulation they make, Anselm had no interest. As Anselm works out his argument, he is acting not as a natural philosopher, but rather as a believing religious man who is using his intelligence in function of his faith.
He does not conceive his argument as heuristic, i.e., as discovering God.
He has already discovered God in his faith. Supposing this discovery, he
finds a metaphysical formula for his faith, which is metaphysically exact
and not logically derivative from faith itself. The non-believer for An-

selm is the non-believer of the order of Original Sin. Before that time man was in loving and familiar contact with God, and that man would have seen the argument lucidly. Of the man of pure nature, a later Scholastic conception, Anselm shows no awareness.

In summary, the following can be said for the mind of Anselm: (1) He does not think that his argument will have value for "fools," i.e., all men born in Original Sin and not cured of their intellectual blindness. (2) He does believe that his argument can be understood lucidly by believers. (3) The argument itself is a fruit of an illumination added to faith, and therefore faith alone does not bring with it an insight into the argument. (4) For the man of pure nature, Anselm has no awareness and he in no way tells us conclusively whether for such a man the argument will give light.

The world contemporary to Anselm was not simply swept off its feet by the argument of Anselm. A reviewer of his book, Gaunilo, a monk of Marmoutier, wrote a clever criticism, manifesting wit and penetration.[40] Since Anselm was arguing against the "fool," Gaunilo says that he will argue in behalf of the fool—*pro insipiente*. Gaunilo in his little review brought out all the objections that were raised against Anselm from that time on. Gaunilo makes some important distinctions: conception, understanding, and existence. By conception he means the dialectical organization of intelligible notes, which is possible even if no reality corresponds to it. By understanding he means a genuine concept in contradistinction to a mere dialectical construction. By existence he means extra-mental existence.

According to Gaunilo, "that than which nothing greater exists" is only a dialectical construction, because different intelligible notes are joined together, but this does not give a genuine concept of God, who is so different from all things that he cannot be constructed from elements derived elsewhere than from himself.[41] Hence for Gaunilo, Anselm is dealing with a mere construct and has no right to attribute this construct to God at all. Secondly, even if it were a genuine concept, it still would be no guarantee that the conceived reality were more than ideal. Genuine concepts do not carry with them the mark of extra-mental existence. Nor does the fact that Anselm's concept deals with the notion of that than which nothing greater can exist change the matter. Gaunilo refers to the lost Atlantis and says that if we define it as the most perfect island con-

---

[40] Gaunilo, *Pro Insipiente*, in *Patrologia Latina*, Vol. 158. The references below are to the numbers of the sections of that work.

[41] *Pro Insipiente*, n. 4.

ceivable, that is no argument that the lost Atlantis exists.[42] He ends with a nice little bouquet to Anselm for evident merits of his work.[43]

Anselm wrote a response to Gaunilo.[44] His response shows the same wit; he begins by saying that he was writing against the fool, but Gaunilo is evidently no fool and moreover, he is a Catholic. Gaunilo therefore is not the adversary of Anselm, even though Gaunilo has made himself an advocate of the fool. However, rather than write against the fool again, he will answer the Catholic.

Against the Catholic he argues promptly: If the concept of God is only a construct, then it follows either that God is unreal or that he is unknowable. Catholic faith rejects either notion. Hence, Gaunilo has reasoned against the faith, and his reasoning must be false. This is the implicit use of the later principle so mighty in Scholastic thought: *contra factum non valet illatio,* reasoning cannot be validly cited against facts.[45]

He then denies all the postulates of Gaunilo. The notion of the being than which nothing greater is conceivable is not a mere construct, for all constructs by their very nature imply possible non-existence, while the notion of the being than which nothing is greater rejects non-existence totally. Hence it is more than a construct, and is a genuine concept—the understanding of reality. Nor can it be argued that because elements of the concept were derived from the non-God, they do not refer to him. On the participation-theory, all elements derived from the real are participated divine reality and are applicable to God.[46] Moreover, a Catholic could never say that elements derived from creatures are inapplicable to God, for Paul taught otherwise in the Epistle to the Romans, I, 20.[47] In other words, Anselm insists that the notion of the being than which nothing greater can be conceived is not a construct, but rather that the non-existent God is obviously a construct, and an invalid one.

With reference to Gaunilo's island Anselm says that the whole observation is not to the point. His argument was not that every concept including real existence as one of its notes makes the concept genuine or that such real existence follows from the concept. His argument is that one and only one notion can do such a thing—namely, the notion of that than which nothing greater can be conceived. Playfully Anselm says that

[42] *Ibid.,* n. 6.
[43] *Ibid.,* n. 8.
[44] The *Responsio Editoris* can be found in *Patrologia Latina,* Vol. 158.
[45] *Responsio,* chapter I.
[46] *Ibid.,* chapter VIII.
[47] *Ibid.,* chapter VIII *ad finem.*

if this concept is that of an island, then the island exists and he, Anselm, will find the island for Gaunilo.[48]

From Anselm's answer to Gaunilo we can make some conclusions as to his mind concerning the validity of the proof.

(1) Given the faith which teaches us the knowability and reality of God, the argument stands, for the objectivity of the God-notion is given us *ex aliunde,* from another source.

(2) The God-concept includes existence not by arbitrary injection of the note, but by its very essence, when conceived as the being than which nothing greater can be conceived.

(3) This position supposes that we do have genuine concepts referring to extra-ideal reality and that among these there is one that is highest. Even if we do not understand all that can be said of its object, yet we can in this singular case see its necessary existence. Experience is not eliminated from the argument, but supposed.

(4) The God-concept is therefore no mere mental construct but a genuine knowledge achievement. The non-existent God is a mere mental construct, illegimately erected so that its illegitimacy becomes evident on examination. To toy with a construct is foolish.

(5) Although ideal reality is generally not of itself a sign of extra-ideal existence, yet in one single case this is true.

Saint Thomas

Something more than a century goes by from the death Anselm (1109) to the birth of Saint Thomas (1224 or 1225), a very productive time in the field of Western thought. In the twelfth century Peter Abelard (1079-1142) performed a great service to Scholastic thought. He brought out into the open and formulated the critical rationalism which was at the heart of it, but which was held down by Platonic and Augustinian illuminationism. Abelard is frequently misunderstood because he is represented as an *outré* rationalist. Such is not the case. In his *Sic et Non* he clearly sustains that, like Anselm, he begins with the faith which is in no way questioned. Nor is there a desire to reconstruct it. In the preface to the work he proposes sober principles of heuristics as applied to the faith: be sure of your text and be sure of the philological analysis of the text, both in scripture and in tradition. In the epistemological battle of those days,

---

[48] *Ibid.,* chapter III. Cf. also chapter V.

he rejected the empirical nominalism of Roscelinus as well as the naïve realism of William of Champeaux, erecting a Platonic conceptualism that is not far removed from the Aristotelian moderate realism of Saint Thomas. His conceptualism and critical spirit did make him water down some of the dogmas, but it was not his a priori intention to do so. The rising rationalism spearheaded by Abelard had to meet stout opposition, and men like Saint Bernard, an ardent illuminationist, were deeply irked by the critical approach of the new men.

In the twelfth and thirteenth centuries we see the rise of the universities as successors to the cathedral schools and monasteries. The crowds attending the new centers and the excellence of the professors naturally gave learning a push upwards and onwards. To aid the new universities a genial work was at hand, the synthesis of theology prepared by Peter Lombard (c.1100-1160). His *Libri Sententiarum* were universally known and the accepted basic text for scholars and masters.

Not only was there life streaming within intellectual Christendom, but there was present the other thing needed for vibrant study—a stimulus from without, which had to be met. Avicenna (Ibn Sina, 980-1037), Averroes (Ibn Rushd, 1126-1198), and Moses Maimonides (1135-1204) in Spain had developed Aristotelianism and their work was brilliant. It was rationalism coupled with empiricism in contrast to the idealistic intellectualism of Plato. The Spanish thought filtered into Christendom and though the schools at first refused the new approach, the rising tide of rationalism found it very congenial. It was the contribution of Saint Thomas to assimilate this non-Christian rationalism into the Catholic outlook of Christendom. He boldly but calmly took Aristotle as the framework for philosophic and theological synthesis, and with this instrument erected a successful Weltanschauung, perhaps the best summation of knowledge for a given moment that the world has ever known.

In his early days at the University of Paris Saint Thomas studied Peter Lombard and, in preparation for the doctorate or mastership, according to the terminology of those days, he explicated the text of the Lombard. Before and after that, he had read many other books, especially the works of Aristotle and Augustine. He knew the works of Anselm too.

In Anselm we saw that thinking was done on two levels and that the levels converge. This Thomas refuses to do. He also thinks on two levels and on either level watches what is happening on the other. Yet he refuses to make the two lines converge, though he keeps them together by making sure that they are parallel.

Anselm had given a theodicy as an independent study. Peter Lombard lightly touches on the theme, but not from an Anselmic point of departure. The Lombard is interested exclusively in theology and consequently restricts himself to the theological method. Among the revealed data is the little theodicy of Saint Paul in the Epistle to the Romans. Hence, Peter Lombard, before entering into the study of the Trinity, gives a sketchy and incomplete outline of a theodicy, based on Saint Paul's argument for a knowledge of God from the visible things of creation. In this outline[49] Peter merely reproduces the thought of the *De Civitate Dei* of Saint Augustine, where a proof for the existence of God is given in terms of causality in the greatest simplicity: things are caused, but the world is a thing, therefore it is caused. The cause of the world is God. A second argument is from change: all things we know change, but change supposes the unchanged. The unchanged is God.

Saint Thomas proposes a theodicy and a natural theology in two places: in the *Summa contra Gentiles* and, in an abbreviated form, in the *Summa Theologica*. The longer natural theology is given in the *Contra Gentiles,* as is only to be expected, because that is a polemic construction of a Catholic world-view against the different adversaries of the faith, the Mohammedans and pagans chiefly. In the *Contra Gentiles* Thomas proposes explicitly his postulates:

(1) A rational approach to the problem of God and God's action on history is possible. (I, 3)

(2) This rational approach has a double method. (I, 3)

(3) Some things concerning God can be known without revelation. (I, 3)

(4) But not all things. (I, 3)

(5) Things not knowable by natural reason left to itself are known by faith, which gives us information beyond the capacities of natural reason. (I, 3)

(6) Even with the things of faith reason has a field. It can refute the arguments of the enemies of faith with certainty, by showing up the fallacy in the opponents' argument. This is possible because faith is never contrary to reason, and therefore, what faith says can be denied only by fallacy of reason. (I, 9; cf. I, 7)

(7) Reason can also give probable arguments for the dogmas of faith, but care must be had lest the adversary who is not a believer think that such persuasive arguments be the reason of our belief, which really rests on the authority of the Scriptures confirmed by miracles. (I, 9)

---

[49] Lib. I, Dist. III, cap. 1 in Migne, *Patrologia Latina*, Vol. 192.

(8) There are many things of faith which can also be known by reason. (I, 4)

(9) The essay of pure reason in matters concerning God is a difficult one for many reasons:

    (a) In some men their intellect is constitutionally formed so as to make philosophic study so unattractive that they cannot do this kind of work. In others the pressure of economic activity prevents the leisure and recollection required for this kind of thinking. There are still others who are just too lazy to go into the intense and prolonged work entailed in this sort of investigation.

    (b) The work is long and infinite patience is required—something very difficult in young people—and only in old age is anything like an adequate vision achieved. Hence there will be only a very few who will go through this kind of investigation.

    (c) Even for such a few, we are faced with the difficulty that men are generally partially in error in their truths. Hence even the best natural synthesis of God and God's action contains fallacious elements. (I, 4)

(10) Hence it is that God in his mercy has told us many things so that by faith we can quickly and securely get the truth. (I, 4)

(11) The supposition is that this revelation is to be found in the Catholic Church. (I, 6)

(12) To accept faith is prudent because of the apologetic arguments derived from the miracles of Scripture and the fulfillment of the Scriptural prophecies. These are confirmed by the miraculous spread of Christianity, rendering evident the credibility of the Scriptural miracles. Besides, miracles are a constant concomitant of Catholicism. (I, 6)

In this catalogue we have expressed the method and rational dynamism of the Thomistic approach to the reality of God. There are in man two intellectual avenues to God: one is faith, and the other is the natural use of reason. Not as in Anselm do the two avenues converge; they always remain distinct but not diverging. Their parallelism is ever perfect, though as a matter of fact, the avenue of faith is longer than the avenue of natural reason. Hence we avoid the absorption of reason into faith, so dear to the illuminationists, and simultaneously we reject the double truth theory of Siger of Brabant (c.1235-c.1282) whereby the two avenues are not united and each goes its own way, even divergently.

The primacy of faith is maintained, and the reason for it is that faith is more perfect than natural reason. Hence, given faith, we have a guide for natural reason, pointing out to it fields of investigation and guiding it in those fields. Thus a reasoned theology is possible. A natural theology is also possible.

The acceptance of faith—the Catholic faith—is prudent. There are miraculous signs that prove that our revelation is from God. Hence an apologetic for faith is at hand—the apologetic of miracles.

We can note at once a difference in the approaches of Thomas and Anselm. Anselm uses reason, but a reason enriched internally by faith. Thomas uses faith as an external guide to reason, which retains its own native limitations which are corrected only externally, namely by the discoveries of faith, with which it can always harmonize.

Although Thomistic reason is thus an autonomous instrument of investigation, yet Thomas recognizes in it definite weaknesses and shortcomings, whereby its need of control by something better is made evident. Among its shortcomings are its subjection to congenital and environmental conditionings which curtail its elasticity, its employment, at times exclusive, for merely temporal goods, and its constant admixture with error, great or small. Therefore, reason alone is a brittle knife with which to carve the form of the real.

With these postulates stated, Thomas at once launches into a theodicetical introduction to a natural theology whch will be the matter of the first book of the *Contra Gentiles* and a good part of the second.

The theodicy of the *Contra Gentiles* will be found in chapters ten to sixteen of the first book. He begins by rejecting the Anselmic argument for the immediate knowledge of the existence of God. He simultaneously rejects the proof from inner finality as an immediate acquisition of the existence of God. (I, 10-11)

Thomas' rejection of Anselm, whom he does not name but whose argument he gives verbatim, rests on the following reasons: (1) Because of environmental suggestion exercised from earliest childhood it is possible to take as self-evident what should be critically examined. (2) As far as human understanding goes, the word "God" does not mean necessary existence, nor yet the highest reality thinkable. This is clear from the pagan conceptions of God, whereby God meant something finite and corporeal. (3) Even if we wish to define God as the being than which nothing greater can be conceived, we are confronted by a double possibility: either that we have conceived a merely ideal reality which does not necessarily imply extra-mental existence or we are supposing without guarantee that there is a being than which nothing greater can be conceived. Hence, though given the extra-ideal reality of God, it is necessarily implied that he exists, yet the mere concept of God does not guarantee that extra-ideal reality, and his existence can be denied without contradiction apparent to the human mind which does not intuit the reality of God.

These Thomistic objections are merely reformulations of the objections of Gaunilo. Thomas evidently was not satisfied with the answers of Anselm to Gaunilo, nor on the other hand does Thomas conceive the Anselmic argument precisely as Anselm did. Thomas does not even oppose Anselm, but proposes the Anselmic argument transferred from the Anselmic plane of discourse to one which Anselm would never have accepted—namely, the plane of autonomous reason not transfused by faith.

What is basic in the semantic doctrine of Thomas is that words of themselves do not objectify the conceptions which can be or are evoked by them. What is more, ideal reality must not be confused with extra-ideal existence. Thirdly, extra-ideal existence must be derived from experience, immediately or mediately. *This last principle is the formulation of Thomistic empiricism, a principle latent and dynamic in all of Saint Thomas' work.* It is, of course, Aristotelian as well, and when drawn further than these thinkers wished, it ends up in absolute empiricism, which we call nominalism or positivism or existentialism.

Thomas rejects the notion of an immediate knowledge of God derived from an analysis of the basic drive in man. (I, 11) He admits that the drive is to beatitude and that beatitude is a god-like state. But a god-like state is not the same as God. However, it is true that from the likeness of effects to their causes, an argument through mediate illation can lead to God. But this involves arguing from causality and there is no immediacy in the analysis.

This argument, if we understand it correctly, states that beatitude of itself and by itself does not bring with it as a contained element the notion of God, though as a matter of fact the state requires God as cause. Only by arguing do we reach the notion of God. In other words, one's perfect happiness does not say nor immediately imply God, even though on other grounds one can argue to his existence. Throughout his total works Thomas makes much of the natural desire for God, but it is clear in this locus that that desire does not illuminate its object, so that the mere desire does not tell what the object is nor give me its nature.

After having rejected the immediate knowledge of God by natural intelligence, Thomas rejects the theory that God can only be known by faith. (I, 12) His arguments are as follows: (1) Logic can proceed a priori, from cause to effect, and also a posteriori, from effect to cause. Hence, given divine effects, we can reason to God. (2) The notion that faith is the sole source of our knowledge of God supposes that natural intelligence can deal only with physics. But metaphysics is also a science and deals with the first subsistence. (3) *De facto* the philosophers have tried to prove the existence of God. (4) Saint Paul makes it clear (*Romans* I, 20) that we can argue from the visible things of creation to the invisible God.

This kind of reasoning is not too incisive. The possibility of arguing from effect to cause may be restricted to arguing to causes of the same order of the effect, and God is certainly not of that order. Secondly, the possibility of metaphysics is the Aristotelian metaphysics, but as we have seen, Aristotle's metaphysics is very much chained to his physics and not vice versa. Thirdly, that the philosophers have tried to prove the existence of God is true, but is it true that they have succeeded? Fourthly, the argument from Saint Paul is proving by revelation that reason can prove the existence of God. Hence it is objectively true that life leads man to God through the use of his intelligence. However, two difficulties present themselves: did Saint Paul conceive his argument precisely as Saint Thomas does? and, is it not strange that to know that you can come to a knowledge of God by nature requires faith to see it?

Having dismissed ontologism and agnosticism, Thomas then launches into a reasoned approach to the knowledge of God. (I, 13) His principal argument is the Aristotelian argument of the unmoved first mover. He gives it at great length and very adequately.

He admits two difficulties with the argument. First, the argument is on the basis of eternal matter in eternal motion. The argument would be more convincing if it supposed the cosmos to have begun in time. Secondly, the whole argument supposes that the first moved thing is a living first sphere which by knowledge moves itself because of its knowledge and love of the unmoved first motor. Many do not admit that the first sphere is animated. (In fact, we can add that in our time no one admits the existence of the spheres.) To this objection Thomas pointed out that metaphysically, independently of the physics involved, the first unmoved motor is necessarily reached.

These two characteristics of Thomas are very enlightening. He admits that the argument would be stronger if it could be shown that the world had a beginning in time. In the *Contra Gentiles* he proves that the hypothesis of an eternal cosmos or eternal matter is not a necessary one. (II, 31-37) He also admits that the arguments given to prove that the world had a beginning are not conclusive but only persuasive. (II, 38) In the *Summa Theologica* he gives his mature judgement on this point and states that it is impossible to prove by reason alone that the world or any finite thing had a beginning. The beginning of the world, like the truth of the Trinity, is a mystery, to be accepted on faith alone. (I, 46, 2)

Needless to say, Thomas does not believe that an eternal world would be an uncaused world. Both in the *Contra Gentiles* and in the *Summa Theologica* he proves that all things derive from strict creation by God. He admits that this is contrary to the teachings of the ancients. (*Contra Gentiles*, II, 15 *ad fin.*, and II, 16 *ad fin.*) He does not name Aristotle, his own master, as holding this opinion, but he does not exclude him, for he says (II, 16) that the ancients could have no idea of creation because they all illegitimately prolonged causality to causality by change of pre-existing matter. In the *Summa Theologica* he argues to the creation of all things on the participation theory of Plato, and makes creation the source of participation. (I, 44, 1)

The weakness of the argument, as Saint Thomas saw it, was that eternal matter suggests uncaused matter. If that were the case, the principle of an unchanged source of change would not give Thomas the kind of a God which he wants, though it would give the god of Aristotle who is only a refined version of the gods of the Epicureans. Such a god is unacceptable to Thomas, the Catholic.

In the *Contra Gentiles* Thomas confirms the argument from the immobile first motor with three other arguments. (1) Aristotle proves that there can be no infinite series of efficient causes, and hence there is a first one. (2) There are degrees of being, as Aristotle insinuates, and hence there is a highest being. (3) As Saint John Damascene points out, the world is obviously governed, a fact that Averroes, the commentator of Aristotle, recognized. (I, 13)

In the *Summa Theologica* where the Five Ways are given, there is another argument, namely, the general law that all potency ultimately supposes pure act. (I, 2, 3) In the *Summa* he continues to think as in the *Contra Gentiles*, to the effect that the argument for Aristotle's unmoved motor is the clearest, but in the *Summa* the other arguments are not treated so cavalierly as in the *Contra Gentiles*. In both books it is clear that Thomas is willing to rest his case on the Aristotelian Prime Motor, which will give him an unchangeable Pure Act, participated by all existent things.

Now with reference to the first efficient cause which Thomas derives from Aristotle,[50] it must be remembered that the unmoved motor in Aristotle is not the efficient cause of anything.[51] All that Aristotle wishes to

---

[50] Aristotle, *Metaphysics*, II, 2, 994a-994b.
[51] *Ibid.*, XII, 1072a and b.

prove is that the first efficient cause is eternal; not that it is divine. Aristotle's first efficient cause, but not creator, is the first sphere. Thomas knew this.

The argument from the degrees of being comes from Anselm, insinuated in Augustine.[52] It does not come from Aristotle, though Thomas cites the *Metaphysics*.[53] Thomas also quotes the fourth book of the *Metaphysics* in his favor but there Aristotle is dealing only with a logical first principle. Thomas seems to be thinking most of Bk. II, 1, 993b *ad fin.*, but here too we are dealing not with causality nor participation but with metaphysical principles of deduction.

The argument from the direction of the world is not Aristotelian at all, nor does Saint Thomas say that it is, though he cites Averroes, the commentator of Aristotle, in his favor. The argument, as we have seen, is Platonic and Stoic. Aristotle's God does not direct the world or govern it.

We have here a slight mystery. Saint Thomas knew Aristotle well. He knew that Aristotle's God is neither a creator nor a governor, but only a first mover. Yet Thomas tries to derive the argument for God's existence under the consideration of efficient causality, participation, and governance in Aristotle and refuses to say that those arguments are from Anselm, Augustine, and Plato. Thomas may not have known what Plato said but he knew both Augustine and Anselm. Thomas was certainly aware that the Anselmic arguments from the *Monologium* pointed differently to God than did Aristotle's reduction of change to the unmoved first mover. The two types of argument do not harmonize, unless we remake Aristotle altogether.

Perhaps some reflections on the mystery might indicate ways of explaining it. Thomas, as a matter of fact, was remaking Aristotle all the time. The Thomistic fusion of causation and participation is his own essay at combining Plato and Aristotle, whether Thomas knew what he was doing or not. Saint Thomas found Aristotle's simultaneous devotion to empiricism and rationalism congenial to his own spirit. Secondly, the adversaries against whom the *Contra Gentiles* was written were principally the Spanish Arabs who were Aristotelians, and he wished to meet them on their own ground. In arguing from Aristotle, Thomas is not restricted to the explicit words of Aristotle. He frequently argues from unvoiced implicits that are not really in Aristotle at all. But this puzzlement would not have disturbed Saint Thomas, for he would have argued that at the bottom of Aristotle there was more truth than Aristotle himself recognized.

---

[52] Augustine, *De Civ. Dei*, VIII, 6; *De Vera Relig.*, XVIII, 35-36; *Conf.*, VII, 11, 17.
[53] Aristotle, *Metaphysics*, Bk. II, 2, 994b *ad fin.*

One other point of the Thomistic theodicy must be stressed. Both in the *Contra Gentiles* and in the *Summa Theologica* we find phrases like the one we met in Anselm. With the argument given, Thomas says: "and this all men understand as God"; "and this we call God"; "and this all men call God." Now this phraseology is interesting because it is not casual, for Saint Thomas repeats it. He does not say that the prime mover is God, but that the God of men, in the meaning given to that word by men, covers the notion of the prime mover, the first efficient cause, the pure act, the greatest being, the governor. In other words, men do not discover God in the arguments; they had him already. In the arguments, they find their God expressed at best partially. Therefore, Thomas does not wish to say that the notion of God had its genesis in the arguments, but rather that the God men believe in can be met under a partial aspect in the arguments. For Thomas, men have a knowledge of God prior to the arguments. Concerning this knowledge he says nothing. It remains an open question whether the God-notion came to men by revelation or some other way. The whole Thomistic attitude to the unaided human intellect, which is subject to so many restrictions and handicaps, and his doctrine that revelation is needed for an adequate conception of God could lead us to believe that for Thomas it was taken for granted that God was met in faith before he was met in reason and that reason under the external guidance of faith can only corroborate what was found by an unreasoned approach to the divine.

This line of reasoning is reinforced by the Thomistic observations on the manner of conceiving God. In the *Contra Gentiles*[54] he insists that God is outside and beyond all categories and class-conceptions, and hence when we use such conceptions—and we cannot avoid it—we must use them *via remotionis,* i.e., by denying of God the categories whereby the finite thing is known as finite. This would seem to make the conception of God to be: God is a no-thing, where thing means finitely bounded.

However, this does not mean a merely negative knowledge. There is something positive at the core of it, and this is possible because of the analogy of being, and the fact of analogous knowledge.[55]

Hence, for Saint Thomas, the human intellect in its conception of God proceeds *via remotionis* and *per analogiam*.[56]

---

[54] *Contra Gentiles,* I, 14. This same doctrine is given in the *Summa Theologica,* I, 12, 12.

[55] *Summa Theologica,* I, 13, 5.

[56] For the whole question as to the validity of the Thomistic proofs for the existence of God, cf. Mortimer J. Adler, "The Demonstration of God's Existence," *The Maritain Volume of The Thomist* (New York: Sheed & Ward, 1943), pp. 188-218. This work is also the fifth volume of *The Thomist,* Jan. 1943.

A question has arisen among Thomistic scholars whether each of the Five Ways is by itself a sure proof of the existence of God, or if all together make a proof; if under all the formalized proofs there rests an unformalized argument.[57]

As Thomas shows clearly, he leans on the Aristotelian argument from change for his starting point in natural theology. The reason is obvious. It makes natural theology easy and rapid. If there is no possibility of change in the first mover, then there is no potency in him. And that is the position of the unchanged mover, for he is unchanged because he is unchangeable. Were he changeable, he would require a mover, since all that is moved is moved by another. Hence there is no potency for change in the first mover. Hence he is pure act. But pure act is all things, because act is restricted only by potency—a non-Aristotelian yet genuine Thomistic concept. The pure act is unique, for plurality implies participation in one act, but the pure act cannot participate, for participation implies potency. The pure act is unrestricted, and hence eternal and omnipresent. The pure act is the source of all being, because all being, in order to be, must share in act, and all act must derive from pure act. Hence God is the creator in the sense of giving the world a temporal beginning. The pure act is all things, and therefore personal and intelligent. The Thomistic natural theology is rapid because it supposes that all being is derived from pure act which must be unique, and because it supposes that act is limited by potency.

The Nominalists

The rationalism in Saint Thomas was evolved by Duns Scotus and it became too thin to suit men. Duns Scotus (c.1265-1308) attacks all problems in the light of what had been taught from the days of Thomas and criticizes the proofs logically. William of Ockham (c.1280-1349) continues this logical criticism but makes it relevant by the metaphysical supposition that reality is unique and individual, making categorization a human construction of experience. This is extreme conceptualism which is identical with nominalism. The nominalists did not develop a new theodicy and, although Ockhamism was a feature of Franciscan thought which earlier in the days of Bonaventure accepted the Anselmic ontological argument, it rejected any a priori approach to God as logically impossible. Nominalist logic proceeds from experience alone.

---

[57] Cf. Adler, loc. cit.

The Reformers

Nominalism paved the way for the Reform. Luther himself was quite opposed to Aristotelianism and his only approach to God was by confident trust. However, the later Lutheran theologians did develop a natural theology which was identical with that of the Scholastics, but this was obviously a sheer borrowing and not a true fruit of the Lutheran appeal to inwardness and to the non-rational seizure of God. In Calvin the situation is slightly different. He has room for a natural theology, but not of a reasoned kind. He supposes that all men have a *sensus divinitatis,* a feeling inducing a search for God, whom they find at least in the revelation of creation. The reasoned natural theology of the Scholastics does not meet with Calvin's approval, for he considers it empty and unworthy speculation. We are not to find out what God is in himself (*quid sit*), but only some qualities or attributes which he has proportionately in common with creatures (*qualis sit*). These are given by revelation—general in creation and in the scriptures, though the latter also contain the particular revelation of redemption. In other words, neither of the sources of Protestant God-orientation found in themselves and their time any need for theodicy. The reality of the Christian God was taken for granted by the age.

Cartesianism

The humanism of the fifteenth and sixteenth centuries along with the split of religious unity made the old forms of reasoning unsatisfactory. The postulates of that reasoning had been not only questioned but also replaced by others. The result was that there was no universally accepted framework for discourse and debate. The man who first felt this lack was René Descartes (1596-1650) and he felt called upon to erect a perpetually valid background for thought in imitation of the methodological framework of mathematics. Methodology in the abstract is a priori and therefore Descartes worked a priori. He was voluntarily restricted to the evident fact of consciousness, and he found it to be an imperfect state, which, however, included the glimpse of a perfect being. Since this glimpse was there, and since it could not be derived from the imperfect, it came from the perfect being himself who inserted it into man's consciousness. The concept of this being included its own existence.[58]

---

[58] Cf. *Discourse on Method,* part 4.

Now we have here a twist on the Anselmic argument and an awareness that the first problem in theodicy is not the proof of the existence of God, but rather the genesis of the God-concept. Descartes answers this question by saying that it is a datum inserted into consciousness by God himself. Given the datum, then the existence of God is evident by analysis.

Logically this is a perfect answer but there remains the question of fact. Is the concept of God an original datum in consciousness? On an analysis of himself, Descartes thought that it was. However, not all investigators came to this conclusion and the observation of Saint Thomas in *Contra Gentiles* (I, 10) comes to mind, namely, that what we accept uncritically from the first days of childhood seems later in life to be obvious, even though it is not.

On the way of proving the existence of God Descartes is sure of himself. His whole position is given to us in the third meditation of the *Meditations of First Philosophy*. Here he does not stress the Anselmic argument so much, as the impossibility of deriving the idea of God except from divine insertion into man. In other words, Descartes relies on two arguments which he combines. The idea of God includes his existence, and this idea cannot be adventitious or factitious, but it must be innate, for it is undeniable. At the same time it must come from God, because nothing less than God could originate such an idea. The perfect outline of the Cartesian theodicy is given to us in the *Principles of Philosophy* (Part I, "On the Principles of Human Knowledge," principles 14-41). Here he gives us many proofs for the existence of God, the first of which is the Anselmic argument (prin. 14). The second is the impossibility of having the idea of God, unless God existed and implanted the idea in us. This argument is from causality using the postulate that no effect can be more perfect than its cause (prin. 17-18). A conclusion of this reasoning is that man is created, for if he were not created, he would be the author of all that he is. But he cannot be the author of his idea of God, and thus he is not the author of himself (prin. 20).

Another proof for the existence of God is human continuance in existence through duration. For man to endure he must be conserved in being. But he has no power in himself to conserve his being, for if he did, he would know it. Hence he is conserved from without. But conservation is the same as creation, and consequently man is created and the creator is God (prin. 21).

The whole nature of God is contained in the idea of God, and we can derive from the idea all the divine attributes, except those which need revelation. Hence we know that God is omniscient, omnipotent, source of all goodness and truth, creator of all things, infinitely perfect (prin. 22). Therefore no special natural theology need be constructed.

It is interesting that Descartes reversed the order of philosophy. In the theodicies that preceded his, a theory of knowledge was already erected before the question of God was treated. In Descartes, God is considered in order to erect an epistemology. He can trust innate concepts because they are from God, the truth, and he can trust all other ideas by comparing them with the innate ideas. Aristotle needed God for physics; Descartes needed him for epistemology.

Cartesianism was not completed in Descartes. Baruch (Benedict) Spinoza looked for an *ens per se,* a being through its own nature, i.e., a substance. If there is only one *ens per se,* then all the rest is accidental to it, and the ultimate subject of any and all reality is God himself. The ultimate cause of Descartes becomes the ultimate subject for Spinoza.

Spinoza in his *Ethics* proves the existence of God by the Anselmic argument.[59] He rings many changes on the argument, but it is always at heart the same one. One such variation is based on the principle that not only being must have its reason, but also non-being. Such a reason of the non-reality of God would be the inner contradiction of the idea, or the influence of an external substance. However, no external substance can be called in to prevent the existence of God, because such a substance by hypothesis would be of an entirely different order than God, but substances do not act out of their order of being. Nor is there any interior contradiction, because God says only perfection. There is no negation in the God-concept, and therefore no contradiction can arise.

Another variation is given on the hypothesis of the existence of finite beings. If God did not exist, then the finite would be more perfect than the infinite and that would be absurd. In this argument we have the position of the Thomistic fourth way—no imperfect being is conceivable or possible, unless the reality of the perfect be supposed. You cannot approximate to perfection, unless perfection is there as a limit. In other words, no meaning can be realized imperfectly unless the reality of the meaning in its pure form is postulated. This kind of arguing will always be *ad hominem.* You admit the reality of finite being, but this admission commits you to the recognition of the reality of the infinite, the absolute, without which your finite beings would be meaningless.

The third constructor of Cartesianism was Gottfried Wilhelm Leibniz (1646-1716). He was one of the most learned and most talented men of human history. In mathematics he was a genius, and along with Newton,

---

[59] Cf. props. 7 and 11, First Part.

an independent discoverer of calculus. His reading was vast both in authors of the past as well as of his time. He wrote equally well in Latin, German, and French. He had travelled much. By constitution he was a pious man and his life was dedicated to the peace of Christendom in terms of political and religious unity. He knew the thought of Descartes which he accepted in its fundamental principles. He also knew the thought of Spinoza, but he found the pantheistic structure of it unsatisfactory. He worked on the extension side of the Cartesian dichotomy: extension and thought. What is more, he reduced the dichotomy to a fundamental unity, the unity of force. His own world-image was in terms of the famous Leibnizian monads—metaphysical atoms each of which was an energy point, capable of consciousness but incapable of acting transiently because of lack of contact with others. The highest monad was God, who fulgurated all other monads and assured unified activity in the monad-universe by introducing a pre-established harmony in the universe.

In France, Cartesian rationalism went to an extreme, producing the naturalist rationalism characteristic of the continental eighteenth century. One of the voices of this movement was Pierre Bayle (1647-1706), the author of the *Dictionnaire historique et critique*. Bayle claimed that faith and reason were in open conflict and contradiction. For Bayle, this fact left only one conclusion: we must drop faith—because Bayle believed in the primacy of reason.

Such a position shocked the believing Christians, and it excited Leibniz to write a reply after the death of Bayle. In this way was born the Leibnizian theodicy, a word that subsequently became a synonym for natural theology. However, Leibniz' theodicy is not a proof for the existence of God nor yet a construction of the concept of God. He wished only to prove that the freedom of man and the foreknowledge and fore-ordainings of God involved no contradiction, nor did the presence of evil in the world—metaphysical, physical, and moral evils—refute the existence of a good, omnipotent God. In this work he proposes his famous theory that this universe is the best of all possible worlds, and that the evils are really goods. More abiding in popularity than this work was Voltaire's burlesque reply in *Candide* in which Doctor Panglos ludicrously justifies the most pitiable evils by the Leibnizian philosophy.

However, Leibniz in the totality of his works does have fugitive reflecttions on theodicy as we understand it today, i.e., the proof of the existence of God. The most interesting is found in *New Essays Concerning Human Understanding*,[60] a work which is an answer to the empiricism of

---

[60] Trans. A. G. Langley (New York: The Macmillan Company, 1896).

Locke. In the fourth book[61] Leibniz reflects on the Anselmic proof as used by Descartes and Spinoza. He makes it clear that the proof is from Saint Anselm, although so many of the writers on the subject had always kept silence on this point.

In the passage referred to, Leibniz professes his own belief in innate ideas. (In fact, his monadology can have no other kind.) He denies the validity of the Thomistic branding of the Anselmic argument as a paralogism. For Leibniz the argument really proves, but the validity of the proof rests on an hypothesis which is not proved by the argument. As Leibniz sees it, the argument says: given the non-contradictory structure of the God-concept, it follows that God exists. This in strict logic is true, and a great advance. Hence, the necessary existence of God is metaphysically certain *in the hypothetical proposition.* The hypothesis of the proposition can be proved with moral certitude by using the Spinozan principle that the non-existence of a conceptual object needs a sufficient reason. If no reason can be shown that the God-concept is contradictory, then morally we are compelled to assent to God's existence. Leibniz adds that more work is required on the analysis of the God-concept in order to show that it is really non-contradictory. In the meantime, the argument proves with moral certitude.

Kant

While the Continent was engaged in naturalistic rationalism, England was developing empiricism in the tradition of Francis Bacon (1561-1626) and John Locke (1632-1704). This tradition reached a definitely high point in David Hume (1711-1776). The English Empiricists did not attack religion, but always showed it respect and even adherence. Consequently, though the Humean empiricism in principle rejected the knowability of the miraculous, which is one of the principal contents of Scripture, and though it more radically deprived the principle of causality of any value other than that of a scientific postulate useful for the unification of empirical observation, yet the English Christians were not deeply disturbed.

However, on the Continent the religious consequences of the Humean doctrine were seen. Ignoring the whole empirical movement in England, Christian Wolff (1679-1754) had prepared a division of philosophy accepted by the schools in his day as well as in ours. He combined the Aristotelian tradition with the new Cartesian-Leibnizian views and offered the following framework: ontology or general metaphysics (Aris-

---

[61] Bk. 4, c. 10, paragraphs 7-9 (Langley, pp. 502 ff.).

totelian first philosophy); special metaphysics cut into three sections—cosmology (Aristotle's physics) or natural philosophy, psychology (Aristotle's *De Anima*), natural theology (Aristotle's metaphysics combined with a Scholastic theodicy); and beyond these divisions, the "practical" disciplines of logic, ethics, and esthetics.

Immanuel Kant (1724-1804) was brought up on this Wolffian philosophy and taught it at Koenigsberg. However, having read the epistemological writings of Hume and Berkeley and having become aware that the Wolffian system did not even envisage the Humean analysis, he resolved to write a definitive epistemology—the never-ending ambition of every age. His solution of the Humean problem was to accept empiricism as basic, but according to a distinction that Leibniz had made in his twist of the ancient Scholastic distinction of a priori and a posteriori. For Leibniz a priori knowledge was knowledge which did not arise out of experience—a respectable position for a man who held the doctrine of innate ideas, and a posteriori knowledge was knowledge which depended on experience—a knowledge hardly consistent with the doctrine that all monads are closed off from all other monads, without so much as a window to look out into the world.

In 1781 at the age of fifty-seven Kant published the first edition of his magnum opus, the *Critique of Pure Reason,* which he corrected and revised in the second edition of 1787, when he was sixty-three years old. With Leibniz he supposes that the function of reason is to concatenate ideas into a unitary system.[62] With Hume, Kant supposes that truth derives from experience.

These two suppositions are combined by a further supposition, namely, that the concatenating work of the reason is done according to the structure native to the intellect. From this structure arises metaphysics which is the expression of the reflective analysis of the mind. The propositions of such a metaphysics are not "true," because truth comes from experience, but they are valuable in so far as they indicate the unavoidable framework to which experience must adjust. In this combination of empiricism and rationalism there is latent the dynamic supposition of all Kant's work, namely, that all knowledge is constructive of its object. Thomistic epistemology supposes that knowledge is constructive of its *concepts* and *judgments,* but this does not mean that knowledge constructs the objects of knowledge, and only means that knowledge is constructive of the means of knowledge. The Kantian notion of knowledge is thoroughly subjective. Empiricism for him means a modification of the subject, and

---

[62] Cf. Leibniz' introduction to the *Theodicy.*

this modification is assimilated in consciousness after a certain fashon dictated by the inner structure of consciousness. What is known is the object constructed by this activity. Kant with no right admits that such an object stands in relation to an object other than the knowing subject, but he denies that it represents it as a vision of the non-subjective object. The real object beyond the subject is thoroughly unknowable, for it enters into consciousness only by a process of construction whose laws derive from the subject and not from the object.

Kant psychologically had a strange compulsion. He was anxious to save religion from the attacks of the atheists by putting God beyond the discussion of reason. He was anxious to prove that the atheists could not prove that there was no God. He did so by insisting that God was not to be achieved by reason, and therefore the atheist was only attacking sophisms used by deists and theists. Proving that the deists and the theists had not proved that God exists, and even using a priori reason to prove that God did not exist, which could be done because of antinomies in reason with reference to the cosmological idea, was all so much silly play. You cannot prove that God exists, just as you cannot prove that he does not.

This commitment of Kant made him deal with natural theology. He does so in many places, but the chief are: (1) the discussion of the cosmological argument in the Second Division of the work, Book II, Chapter 2, entitled "The Antinomy of Reason," section 2, the fourth antinomy,[63] and section 9;[64] (2) the Second Division, Book II, Chapter 3, "The Ideal of Pure Reason,"[65] in which part Kant tries to show the invalidity of the proofs of the existence of God.

Kant declares that there are only three rational proofs of the existence of God: (1) the ontological argument, which is Kant's denomination of the Anselmic argument. Kant says nothing of Anselm but refers only to Descartes. (2) The cosmological argument, which is the Kantian denomination of the argument from causality. (3) The physico-theological argument, which is Kant's way of speaking of the argument from the order in the world.

According to Kant these are the only arguments from reason which are possible. In his cosmological argument he includes both the argument from the prime mover and from the series of efficient causes. In his ontological argument he includes the argument from act and potency, and

[63] Cf. Immanuel Kant, *Critique of Pure Reason*, trans. F. Max Müller, 2nd ed. rev. (New York: The Macmillan Company, 1934), pp. 370 ff.
[64] Müller translation, pp. 419 ff.
[65] *Ibid.*, pp. 459 ff.

the argument from the degrees of being. Consequently, Kant rejects all of the Thomistic Five Ways.

Kant's position on these arguments is quite complicated. Hence, it is quite naïve for non-Kantian philosophers to affirm blithely that Kant once and for all destroyed the rational arguments for the existence of God. Given the Kantian epistemology—a rather weird thing—he has destroyed the arguments, but there is none today who is an undiluted Kantian.

With reference to the ontological argument, Kant advances the objections made by Saint Thomas in the thirteenth century, and previously by Gaunilo in the eleventh. The objections are stronger in Kant because he supposes that a priori reasoning makes absolutely no affirmation about reality, but only concerning the possibility of experience. Where there is no experience there is no affirmation of reality. For Kant, the ontological argument is the highest ideal of pure reason, namely, the reduction of all synthesizing functions to the total unity. Such a reduction shows up the dynamism of reason, but absolutely nothing about reality. The ontological argument shows up a possible concept, possible in the sense that it conforms to the pushes of the mind, but not necessarily objectively possible. Hence nothing whatsoever is given us by the idea of God except an empty concept.

The cosmological argument derives from the idea of a unified universe, but this idea is not derived from experience but from the unifying tendency of the mind. "World" may mean two things: the objects which we meet in experience, or, the unification of the many empirical objects made without reference to experience, since we cannot experience the whole. Causality is a temporal-spatial device useful for organizing the constructed percepts of experience. It has no other function and, therefore, it is illegitimate to use it with reference to an unempirical object like the "world," taken in the second meaning above. Causality functions within the world; it can never take you beyond the world. Nor does it discover the God-concept, which is only discovered by the ontological argument. Therefore, when in the cosmological argument reason departs from experience and retreats to the realm of its own concepts, it is falling back into the ontological argument which alone gives us the God-concept.

The physico-theological argument can only show us order in a contingent world. It does not do more. It argues to God by reflecting on contingence, which is nothing but the cosmological argument. This in turn introduces us to the ontological argument, and that was shown to be fallacious.

Since there are only three rational arguments for the existence of God
and these reduce to the ontological argument, which is a sophism, there
is no valid rational proof for the existence of God.

However, it is not the intention of Kant to resign himself to a life
without God. In the *Critique of Pure Reason* he outlines the thought
which will be the theme of the next work, the *Critique of Practical Reason*.[66] (Practical reason is no reason at all, but the will, rationally considered, in its moral behavior.) Moral behavior is necessary for man, because the categorical imperative, "the voice of conscience," is a prime
datum of human life. The *postulates* of this imperative are that man has
freedom and personal immortality, and that God exists as a moral intelligence who organizes the universe to permit moral behavior with its
proportioned happiness consequents. Thus moral action gives a conviction where pure reason cannot.

The importance of Kant's observations on natural theology and theodicy must be borne in mind. Until recently it was glibly stated by all
critics of theodicy that Kant had demolished all rational approach to
God. Even today this kind of affirmation is made by some. However,
Kant did not destroy the validity of anything. All he did was to give empiricism a new value, greater than had been done before. He still kept
reason, but he made it a metaphysic of thinking, which was never heuristic[67] but merely constructive of the only heuristic there is, experience.
This position was a new one in philosophy. Plato and Descartes, thanks
to a belief in spontaneous intellectual intuitions native to the mind,
made reason heuristic, and by its discoveries all other discoveries were to
be controlled. Aristotle and Thomas made experience the source of all
knowledge, but they found a metaphysical core in the empirical real. In
all these systems metaphysics is real. In Kant it was not real, but only
subjective conditioning, but a conditioning which was inevitable and
universal to all men. Metaphysics for Kant was a regrettable law, but
it was a law which had to be followed, provided that it was not used beyond experience.

The objective invalidity of metaphysics made room for the dethrone-
ment of metaphysics, but the positivists were not satisfied with that alone.
They denied that man was inevitably tied to metaphysics. Constructions
for Kant were necessary according to an innate law. For the positivists
constructions were free. Man made them as he pleased. The necessity that

---

[66] Cf. *Critique of Pure Reason*, "Method of Transcendentalism," Chapter 2, section
2, "Of the Ideal of the Summum Bonum," Müller transl., pp. 645 ff.

[67] heuristic: serving to discover something.

Kant saw in metaphysics, according to the positivists, was the necessity attaching itself to grammar, not to thinking. The principle of contradiction is valid, not because we cannot think otherwise, but because the word "is" has a definite grammatical law for its usage. Metaphysics is valid only in the form of logic, which permits the substitution of one symbolic expression for another, according to certain linguistic rules, which rules can be changed. This more thorough rejection of metaphysics pushes the positivists into frank and open hostility to Kant, who kept the necessity of metaphysics even though he denied its objective validity.

There are two fundamental contradictions in Kant's analysis of knowledge. First of all, his supposition that there is a real objective X, unknown and unknowable, but yet the referent of the subjective construct called the phenomenon, is wholly gratuitous and supposes a knowledge of more than phenomena, although Kant explicitly states that we know only phenomena. If we cannot know X, by what right can we say anything about it, including its reality? Secondly, Kant begins his analysis by an intuition of knowledge, which intuition he puts beyond the restrictions of constructive laws. There is, therefore, in the Kantian system an initial insight into objective reality just as it is. It is true that Kant gives only one kind of object to this intuition, namely, the subjective activity of the mind, yet his anti-intuitionist epistemology begins with a profound faith in the intuition of the mind, at least in one narrow area.

These two contradictions were discovered in Kant's lifetime. The transcendental idealists—Fichte, Schelling, and Hegel—decided that they would drop the contradictions. They were willing to limit the mind to the subjective order, but they promptly denied that there was any other order. George Wilhelm Friedrich Hegel (1770-1831) made being identical with thought, and made thought the self-consciousness of reality. Unlike Kant, Hegel refused to limit the validity of thinking, but accepted it wherever it led. In Kant there was no room for God in a rational philosophy. In Hegel there was room only for God, and that is what made philosophy different from all other forms of thinking. Hegel accepted the Anselmic argument as valid and dismissed the objections of Gaunilo, Saint Thomas, and Kant as irrelevant, because they did not see that thought and being are one. If there is a human concept of God as existent, then God is existent, because concepts are only the real rendered conscious. Any appeal to an extra-mental reality is an appeal to something meaningless. On this ground Hegel considers Kant as quite blind to the force of the Anselmic argument.

Positivism and Existentialism

Kantianism, in its original form or in its developed form in Hegel, lost its appeal for Europe in the last quarter of the ninteenth century. Positivism was rising in different guises. John Stuart Mill, Herbert Spencer, and Thomas Huxley developed it in England. Auguste Comte produced a naïve scheme of it in France. The theorisers of science in France and the Germanies, men like Ernst Mach, gave it a more thorough and more precise formulation. Two Americans, Charles S. Peirce and William James, gave an American twist to positivism under the name pragmatism.

By positivism we mean an empiricism that is hostile to metaphysics. There are degrees to such hostility, but its minimum degree is the refusal to accept any validation for propositions except experience. Of course, hostility to metaphysics is itself a metaphysical attitude, but that does not stop it from being an historical reality even though there is a latent contradiction in it. Positivism need not be materialistic, and in fact the modern positivist does not wish to be materialistic, and if he professes materialism, he will insist that it is a non-reductive materialism, i.e., the matter which is the basis of experience is not homogeneous nor is its only activity mechanical. Mechanistic materialism is as dead as the dodo. Positivism can be religious, even intensely religious, but it will not look for help from metaphysics. For the positivist a religion of metaphysics is nonsense. No matter how religious the positivist be, one limit necessarily hampers his religiosity—the incapacity of defining God objectively. God is not experienced outside the mystical state, which is an experience not subject to the criticism of public fact.

We can indicate three forms of positivism active and influential in our time. There is the Dewey type of naturalism, called by him instrumentalism. This theory rejects metaphysical thinking as naïve and illusory and wishes to substitute for it the method of science, the way of experimentation through trial and error, illuminated by theoretical constructs freely made, where the dynamism is a desire for a better society in terms of the fuller well-being of the members—all members—of society. Religion as an aid to such well-being is not rejected, but God, the object of religion, must be constructed and constantly reconstructed in favor of society. Since God cannot be experienced, there is no reality of God in himself.

Logical positivism is the purest form of positivism.[68] In a man like Richard von Mises it takes on the framework of a transcendental philosophy. Experience is the only knowledge. Metaphysics is a system combining semantic tautologies and plain nonsense. Religion can have a place in this framework as long as it is recognized as a value pursuit and not a search for reality. Its function will be morality. Logical positivism supposes that all meaningful propositions are expressions of experience or the expressions of semantic rules whereby one formula of experience can be substituted for another formula. Philosophy studies the laws of substitution. In other words, philosophy, instead of being a metaphysics, is only logic, a logic where inference means substitution of one formula for another according to the rules of language, the language at hand, or better, a language created by a group of men interested in a certain field of experience. Questions of idealism, realism, materialism are meaningless questions and are to be ignored. They derive from the illusion that reality has a definition other than semantic. Knowledge is mental construction of experience according to a given framework of conventional discourse. This is quite Kantian in its tendency, but un-Kantian in its rejection of an innate a priori.

Continental positivism for the moment is existentialist. This form of positivism is voluntaristic. The basic truth for existentialism is that man is a drive. Intellect is one manifestation of this drive; it is not an insight into being but rather an instrument for the acquisition of the good. Existentialism has as many forms as there are existentialists, but all will agree that the real is the existent subject as subject. This makes reality exclusively singular and exclusively existential. The subject is a closed-in monad who is his own law without guidance or help to be derived from the other monads. The thoroughgoing existentialist thus denies the reality of God, objective law, and objective meaning. The religious existentialist makes an exception in favor of God, the object of the drive in man. The religious existentialist can even erect a metaphysic, but it derives not from the study of general reality, but from the drive experienced in the human subject.

It is clear from this rapid—and obviously incomplete—description of positivism that it cannot have a religion from metaphysic, because of the necessary hostility to that kind of thinking. It is also clear that atheism is more congenial to positivism than a theistic vision. Yet in spite of this, we have some interesting developments in modern positivism.

[68] For some works of positivists and analysts on the question of the existence of God see the listings in the bibliography under Positivism and Analysis.

Karl Jaspers, one of the outstanding existentialists, holds for God, and makes God one of the high contents of philosophy, and yet he praises Kant for having shown up the inadequacy of the metaphysical proofs of the existence of God.[69] Gabriel Marcel is both a Catholic and an existentialist.

More interesting still is the movement of existential theology as developed by Karl Barth, Emil Brunner, and Paul Tillich, to which names should be added the American exponent of this kind of thinking, Reinhold Niebuhr. These men are all Protestant theologians. They show a deep awareness of the reality of God and a whole-hearted submission to him. Yet they are vociferous foes of natural theology.[70] They all reach God in God's revelation of himself. For Barth and Brunner this revelation takes place in the reading of the Scriptures. For Tillich it can take place in man's reflections on the world and himself, but when it takes place it is not a reasoning on these things but an ecstatic recognition of the ground of these things.

Against this modern objection to theodicy the Catholic Church takes a firm stand. Pius XII says:

> Notoriously, the Church makes much of human reason in the following connections: when we establish beyond doubt the existence of one God, who is a personal Being; . . . But if reason is to perform this office adequately and without fear, it must be trained on the right principles; it must be steeped in that sound philosophy which we have long possessed as an heirloom handed down to us by former ages of Christendom. . . . What is the character of this philosophy which the Church thus recognizes and receives? It upholds the real, genuine validity of human thought-processes; it upholds the unassailable principles of metaphysics—sufficient reason, causality and finality; it upholds the possibility of arriving at certain unalterable truth.[71]

This is of course the position of the Vatican Council.

> The same holy Mother Church holds and teaches that God, the beginning and end of all, can be certainly known by the natural light of human reason from the things of creation.[72]

---

[69] Cf. Karl Jaspers, *The Perennial Scope of Philosophy*, trans. Ralph Manheim (New York: The Philosophical Library, 1949), pp. 30-33.

[70] Cf. Paul Tillich, *Systematic Theology*, Vol. I (Chicago: University of Chicago Press, 1951), pp. 119-120 and 204-210.

[71] *Humani Generis*, August 12, 1950, paragraph 29, Knox translation. Cf. paragraph 3.

[72] Sess. III, cap. 2 de fide, DB1785.

N. B. James Collins has given an excellent treatment of natural theology in the modern period in his book *God in Modern Philosophy* (Chicago: Henry Regnery Company, 1959). A recent original essay in natural theology can be found in the work of Paul Weiss, *Modes of Being* (Carbondale: Southern Illinois University Press, 1958).

8

A Consideration of the Natural Proofs for the Existence of God

•

The Philosophical Arguments

We have rapidly examined the arguments that philosophy in its long history has made in favor of the existence of God, and the reflections that philosophy has made on those arguments. Let us summarize them.

(a) There are first of all the famous Five Ways of Saint Thomas which may be indicated as follows:[1]

(1) Change implies the unmoved First Mover.
(2) Efficient casuality in nature implies an uncaused First Cause.
(3) The contingency of things, i.e., the non-necessity of their being, shows up a Necessary Being to explain the existence of the contingent.
(4) Degrees in being show up the Perfect Being.
(5) The order in the world shows up a Designer.

The first argument is identical with that of Aristotle. The second was proposed by the Stoics and used in his own fashion by Saint Paul, echoing the meager theodicy of the Old Testament; it was also proposed by Anselm. The third argument is implicit in the Platonic doctrine of ideas and is insinuated by Anselm. Argument four is implicit in Plato, Augustine, and Anselm.

The first three ways are arguments from regress, not necessarily to be proposed as regress in time, but certainly regress in terms of logical priority. The regress argument in any of its forms can be simplified into the

---

[1] *Summa Theologica*, I, 2, 3.

following proposition: the relative to be understood, requires a prior even though implicit recognition of the absolute. It can be stated another way: the relative is unthinkable without positing an initial absolute.

Likewise, the first three ways all claim to be existential arguments—a posteriori. They start with the admission of the existence of the relative.

The fourth way is Platonic—the reduction of all being to an absolute one. It looks like the Anselmic ontological argument, but Thomas did not identify the two arguments. It is different from the ontological argument because it begins with the *existence* of being, less than perfect being. Therefore, as Thomas sees it, it is an existential argument and he does not fall into inconsistency by using it after his rejection of the ontological argument.

(b) Besides proposing five arguments, Thomas rejects two others which he knew from the writings of older philosophers: (1) The Argument of Anselm which is perhaps implicit in Plato and Augustine, and explicit in Bonaventure, Descartes, Spinoza, and proposed with modifying restrictions by Leibniz, Hegel, the ontologists (Gioberti and Rosmini) and Tillich; (2) The argument of the human need of God as the source of ultimate human happiness. This argument is in Saint Augustine and in the immanentistic Catholic apologetes after Blondel. It is also found in all believing existentialists of our time.

(c) Besides these seven arguments considered by Saint Thomas, there were and are others.

(1) The Platonic argument from the consent of all peoples.
(2) The Kantian non-metaphysical derivation of God from morality.
(3) The miraculous break-through of God into history.
(4) The argument from Carnot's second law of thermodynamics. This argument is derived by applying the Aristotelian argument of the Unmoved Mover to the universe as subject to the law of entropy (the second law of thermodynamics), according to which any closed system will level its energy to zero. Since it must come to a static state at some point, it must have had a beginning as an active energy system, it is subject to a finite period of active energy. Hence, the universe had a beginning, and hence it had a motor prior to it from whom its motion is derived.

The argument for God's existence through revelation is not a metaphysical argument to all, and therefore does not concern us. The argument from mysticism, i.e., extraordinary experience of God as an empirical object, is not a metaphysical argument and it need not be considered.

Criticism of the Metaphysical Arguments

All the arguments we have catalogued have been attacked by philosophers and logicians. We have already seen such attacks and the grounds for them. We have seen that Kant reduces all the theodicetical arguments to three: order, regress, and the ontological argument, and he insists that all arguments employ the ontological argument for their final conclusion. Hence, for Kant there is only one argument for the existence of God—metaphysics, and it is invalid. We have also seen that Kant's observations are valid only if we accept his metaphysical epistemology, which no one does. On the entirety of that epistemology rests the Kantian refutation of the arguments for the existence of God. Since we do not subscribe to Kantian epistemology, we cannot blithely accept the Kantian destruction of the metaphysical arguments for the existence of God, and we must examine them in the light of a metaphysics and epistemology more acceptable than Kant's.

I think that we can eliminate the four arguments not mentioned by Saint Thomas as not stringently conclusive. The consent of the peoples is an argument only if we suppose that the human mind in the genus is by structure acquisitive of truth. Such a supposition supposes an intelligent structurer of the mind. Hence, the argument really supposes the existence of God, before it comes to its premises. The argument is, however, not without persuasive force, because the principle that "forty million Frenchmen can't be wrong" has a normative value in human behavior. However, the force of the principle is not strictly metaphysical. It is a fact that forty million Frenchmen have been wrong, and even if they were never wrong, there is nothing in numbers that will give to a large group an assured insight into truth, though it is a human fact that individual fallibility is more probable than group fallibility. Other principles must be brought in, and they will always involve one of the seven arguments proposed by Saint Thomas.

Secondly, the Kantian derivation of God from the moral drive is not metaphysical in the Kantian context. It can be rendered metaphysical by applying to the fact of moral drive the regress argument, or the ontological argument.

Thirdly, the miraculous events in history are not miraculous if there is no God. To be miraculous, it is necessary to know that God exists, for a miracle is a God-produced event freed in history. To call an event God-produced means that you already know God and accept his action at least as possible in the universe.

Fourthly, the argument from entropy is not valid in metaphysics. It has a provisional validity in physical science, and it makes no pretence at absolute and universal applicability. Its persuasive approach is an *argumentum ad hominem* but logically impotent. All arguments for the existence of God derived from physical theories are as weak as those theories, and the theories were never built for the heavy duty of metaphysical thinking.

This brings us to the consideration of the seven arguments mentioned by Saint Thomas. Of the Five Ways, at least three are forms of regress thinking. The fourth way can also be considered a regress argument, and Saint Thomas does so consider it. In the first, the regress is from motion to unmoved mover. In the second, there is a regress from efficient cause which is caused to an uncaused efficient cause. In the third, there is a regress from potency to pure act. In the fourth, there is a regress from imperfect being to the perfect being, and the argument rests on the participation theory of Plato. By this theory, all objects of a class or quasi-class share in the reality of a prime member who constitutes the reality of the class and participates to x realities his own peculiar reality. This is not quite the same as causality, unless causality itself be understood as a manifestation of participation, or a synonym for it. If the argument is not understood in this way, it is the Anselmic Argument, which Thomas rejects. Let it be remembered that the argument has regress value only on the hypothesis of Platonic participation. In Aristotle, classes are formed by realities which are what they are without participation. The basis of classification is a form, individual in all members, and universal and hypostatic only through abstraction. In Plato the universal is primarily a concrete unity, transfused into many existent subjects. In Aristotle the universal is a mental construct justified by the identical intelligibility of diverse objects. How this is possible Aristotle does not explain.

Let us begin our criticism of the Five Ways with an analysis of the fifth way. The argument proceeds from a consideration of non-rational nature, where at least a relative uniformity of class activity is noted. The effect of the uniformity is the obvious welfare of the group. Such uniform action in non-rational agents unto their own good, indicates an intelligently predetermined direction of the activity of these agents, which must reduce to God.

This argument has many forms. Plato used it. It can be found in the Book of Job. The preachers use it with great effect. The preacher's trick is to describe the universe as a clock, which needs an intelligent clock-maker. Now there are tacit postulates in the argument. For Thomas, an intelligent predetermination of action in a finite agent meant the pre-vision and election of the consequent of such action by a being capable of such prevision and election. Given, therefore, intelligent predetermina-tion in non-intelligent agents, the primal intelligent determiner is given. This is the modern concept of teleology. However, this was not the con-cept of Aristotle. For him, predetermination is physical by means of a con-stituent end-seeking principle which he appropriately called entelechy, the inner end-principle. Any being in nature has such a principle and therefore acts in search of its end. However, for Aristotle this principle was not God-made but spontaneous in nature. Nature was intrinsically rational, even though many of its elements were not intelligent. Conse-quently all that Aristotle taught was that every natural agent is intrinsi-cally determined to a set action, and since the universe is rational, i.e., conforms to the laws of reason, the determination is always rational, but spontaneously so. No prevision is supposed and no extrinsic determin-ation. Aristotle's doctrine is the same as that of scientific method: there is some determination in natural agents which can be expressed in accord to the laws of reason. By this principle so understood no God can be derived from the recognition of uniformity and adjustment. This is why the principle of teleology so strong in Aristotle never led him to God, nor could it. Aristotle believed that nature was rational, not in the sense that an intelligence made it so, but only in the sense that a human intelligence would find the structure of his thinking and the structure of the world identical. Natural determination was therefore for him rational determi-nation without any intelligent being involved in predetermining the order of events. The mere fact of uniformity and adjustment of activity in the universe does not metaphysically prove the existence of God. It could be necessary in nature by the very structure of nature.

This was seen by the Scholastic champions of the teleological argument. They did not derive the existence of God immediately from the fact of uniformity and adjustment in the world. They proceeded further. Uni-formity and adjustment of contingents, when these contingents are many and the uniformity and adjustment are necessary, implies that the uniformity and adjustment cannot be explained by the nature of the agents, for the necessary can never be explained by the contingent. Hence, the teleological argument for the Scholastics was really this: the necessary uniformity and adjustment of contingent agents implies a necessary cause. Now when presented thus, the argument is no longer a new argument, but the argument of regress in terms of contingence and necessity, which is the Thomistic third way. Unless the argument be understood in this fashion, it will not prove the existence of God.

The clock and the clock-maker are not valid parallels. If a human being who had no concept of God but had an average knowledge of the workings of nature, found a clock on a desert isle, and had the certainty that no man had ever been on the island, and that the island was perfectly isolated from human activity in its entire history, such a man would have no grounds in logic for concluding that the clock was made by an intelligent agent. There is nothing in a clock that is not "natural." Every part is taken from nature, and the activity of the clock is natural. The man would be struck by the strangeness of the object. In all his acquaintance with nature, he would never have seen anything like it. But the novelty of the phenomenon in terms of his experience does not prove that nature in a novel set of circumstances could not produce it. It is true that the human being, because of his habituation to nature acting in a certain pattern, would jump to the conclusion that the clock was made by an intelligent agent. But he would be jumping at a conclusion and not deriving it with logical necessity from the mere presence of the clock. Even with this conclusion he would at most arrive at an intelligent agent, but not an agent that was beyond nature. If the clock is the sum-total of the universe then, even in the hypothesis of an intelligent agent, we still do not have an agent that is not homogeneous with the effect, even though he would be outside of the closed system of the universe. Zeus or Plato's Demiurge who made the world were not themselves the High Divinity which is God.

Consequently, concerning the fifth way, we can say that teleology if understood only as rational determination of natural activity—Aristotelian teleology—does not prove the existence of God. If understood as the determination of natural activity by an intelligence acting in terms of foreknowledge and election, it will be useless, because uniformity and adjustment of themselves do not demand such a teleological concept. Teleology in nature, which empirically is only uniformity and adjustment, can point to an intelligent first cause only by appealing to the instability and contingence of the agents in an activity that is stable and universal. This is arguing not from teleology but from contingence, and teleology is only cited as an experienced instance of necessity as its source. The argument is not invalid *per se*. It is only as valid as the regress from contingence to necessity. In other words, the fifth way is not an independent proof, but only another formulation of the regress argument.

Let us see the regress argument. Its formulation in terms of the First Mover simply reduces change to non-change as a source. It does not deal with *causa essendi* (cause of being) but only *causa fiendi* (cause of becoming), for the First Mover does not give *esse* (being) but only *esse tale* (being such) through the instrumentality of change. The First Mover only changes the existents; he does not strictly make them. What is more, he is only the intentional incentive urging an inferior to act physically. His contribution to the change is indirect. Because he is, other things act in their way, but he does not act on them at all. The Prime Mover in this kind of reasoning is thus only a primal condition of a series of changes, or even of a single change. To hypostatize such a condition seems to be logically invalid, unless it is supposed that the Prime Mover is also and necessarily the *causa essendi* of the things changed. We think that such a supposition must be made, even though Aristotle did not make it. Change is a mark of contingence, and contingence is the mark of potency. Potency can have no existence unless it be given to it from without. A possible is always a possible, but by that fact it is not an actual. The addition of actuality to a possible supposes an actuality beyond the order of the possibles, which are a metaphysical quasi-class and not mere logical postulates. What is more, possibility itself, which has no actuality, supposes actuality for its own intelligibility. The possible is that which can exist. Without existence, possibility cannot be conceived. You must conceive existence along with it. What is more, the possible, to be such, must stand in relation to the existent which can share actuality with it. Only because man is an existent can he conceive the possible, for he gives it the actuality of his actual mind. If that man himself is more of a possible than an actuality, and his impermanence shows this to be the case, then we must fall back on the Pure Act, without which no possible can be conceived. The Pure Act is the necessary condition for all thought, and through thought reality comes to man. The Pure Act is thus the *prius* of all thinking and, in man, thinking is the norm of reality.

It is clear from these reflections that the first four ways of Saint Thomas are not radically different arguments, but are rather the same argument considered from different angles of respect. Change involves not only *causa fiendi* but also raises the question of the *causa essendi,* and that raises the question of the nature of contingency, which involves the notion of Pure Act or Highest Being. The first four ways are steps toward a unified view of reality. They represent an ascending progress where the following argument always meets with the difficulty which can be proposed against the prior argument. Any one of the first four ways supposes the others and as far as we can see, the fifth way needs the third way. Hence, the Five Ways are four steps in one complex argument with two points of departure: either you begin from the multiplicity of the universe as indicated by change, or you begin with the unity of nature as indicated by uniformity and coherence. Both of these beginnings are existential beginnings.

The arguments of the Five Ways are thus logically coherent and inescapable, given certain epistemological suppositions. First of all it is supposed that there is a real distinction between possible and actual, i.e., essence and existence. Secondly, it is supposed that an essence-existence composite receives or shares the existence from a Pure Existent of which it can be said that its essence is its existence, or that it has no essence other than its existence. Thirdly, it is supposed that essence and existence are quasi-classes of reality, which itself is an analogous term. Hence, they can be attributes and not mere logical modes of discourse. Fourthly, it is supposed that reality is met only in thought and according to the structure of thought, so that the laws of thought and the laws of reality are identical and not merely correlative. Fifthly, it is supposed that any criticism of the object of mind by comparison with an unthinkable object is nonsense. Sixthly, it is supposed that the mind, though constructive of the act of knowledge, is not constructive of the object of knowledge, so that knowledge objects must be accepted as data of the real, which cannot be questioned without the denial of the undeniable, knowledge. This comes down to the affirmation that knowledge is an intuition of the real, not in itself but in its assimilation through thought. Seventhly, it is supposed that empirical receptivity is not formal knowledge until it is organized by the basic intuitions of the mind. Hence, any comparison of the object of thought with a supposed pure empirical object is nonsense.

Now these seven suppositions—let us not call them postulates, a term which too often means *fiat* principles of discourse—are not shared by all philosophers. They involve an epistemological realism too heady for men not submissive to the core of their being, thinking.

Aristotle did not share the suppositions. He did not believe that the mind received its final object, but that it made it. The construct was valid for him, because he thought that it was produced in terms of a reference-parallelism between thought-object and real-object. For Aristotle there never was an intuition of any reality, except the reality of thought, which was different in structure and objectivity from the reality beyond thought. The experienced was the real and what was thought was not wholly real but quite parallel to it.

Kant obviously did not share the suppositions. For him the real was unknowable and in its place we substitute something else; this substitution is licit provided that it refers to an empirical object. Metaphysical laws were for him conditions for constructing an object out of blind experience. They had no other value and it was quite regrettable that they were around at all, but we were saddled with them and had to accept them. The best that we could do was to pay as little attention to them as possible.

No positivist, no matter what be his particular brand of positivism, shares the Thomistic suppositions. In its rudest formula, positivism can be boiled down to the Missouri principle: Seeing is Believing. If the positivist cannot be given an object in experience, he quite calmly though stubbornly denies that the object is there. He may be prudent about it and simply refrain from making any statement concerning such a thing, but until you show it to him, he simply refuses to admit it is there. It is the positivism of our age and the unphilosophical attitude of the multitude which makes the Thomistic arguments useless in debate. A man of common sense, as he loves to call himself, simply considers the whole argument from metaphysics so much blather. He does not even do it the honor of examining it. He rejects the approach as soon as he is told that the argument proceeds from a principle that is not "Seeing is Believing."

What of the two arguments that Saint Thomas rejects? Let us first deal with the Anselmic argument. Saint Thomas rejects it only if it be considered a mathematical proof. Since mathematics by its own structure can make no affirmation concerning the existential world from which it prescinds, the very word "existence," for the mathematician or what is practically the same thing, the logician, does not refer to existence at all. Mathematician and logician deal exclusively with the essence and for them the word "is" is only an equals sign. Consequently, any type of mathematical or sheerly logical proof of the existence of God is impossible for the simple reason that existence is excluded from this type of reasoning.

However, the Anselmic argument need not be considered as a mathematical proof, even though Spinoza so used it. Existence is something which is beyond pure essence and cannot be reduced to it at all, though essence itself can and must be reduced to existence. Essence is a legitimate approach to existence, and by it a finite mind adequately manages the real, especially the finite real. If therefore we start with existence as interpreted by essence, the Anselmic argument takes on a new dynamism. Kant was quite right when he said that the Thomistic proofs included the Anselmic argument and that the Five Ways which are only two ways rest on the Anselmic argument. However, for Thomas, existence was the starting point and not mere postulational deduction. Existence is intuited, but this intuition, unexpressed by any essence, can only be grasped in an essence framework. Just as existence is an undeniable datum, to which we must submit willy-nilly, so too the essence-skeleton in existence must be accepted. Existence is not amorphous or formless. Its intelligibility is the essence, at least for the human mind. Thomas found that existence, that undefinable aspect of reality which is its first face, became analogously intelligible by the Anselmic argument. It was intelligible in no other way. The problem of existence could not be solved by ignoring it but, once admitted, it could be understood by the essence approach. Thus there is nothing illegitimate in the Anselmic argument, provided it be an analysis of existence and not merely an analysis of essence. To the positivist, Thomas says simply that experience gives you only becoming, but becoming is unintelligible unless it supposes *esse*. It is for Thomas a sign of mental lethargy, or worse, a sign of crass materialism, to stay with existence on its becoming level. He was pessimistic enough to think that most men would not get off this level.

Saint Thomas in the same way was not unfair to the argument from the *desiderium naturale* (natural desire) for God, or as the modern existentialists would say, man's groping for transcendence. Saint Thomas simply stated a truism in observing that impulse is not knowledge, nor is it necessarily accompanied by a knowledge. Saint Thomas quite willingly admitted that because of the impulse man could be led to knowledge, but emphasized that knowledge is a by-product of impulse. The impulse would have to be analyzed in terms of existence, and only in that framework would it show up intelligibly the object of desire. Just as Thomas refused to deal with a pure-essence approach to God, so he refused to accept a blind impulse to God. The real was intelligible and the knowledge of God is a problem of intelligibility, not drive. The drive is not only to God, but also to intelligence, and without the drive the question of God would not arise. The drive therefore is the pre-intellectual condition for the question, but it is not the question itself.

This doctrine will furnish an answer to the question how did Saint Thomas explain the discovery of the concept of God. He does not propose this question formally, but it is implicit in all his work.

Given the impulse to God in an intelligent agent, intelligence indirectly but surely would be driven to the God-concept. For Thomas it would be impossible for man not to come to the question—what is the source and end of all things—and as he says, this is what man calls God. Hence, to the question—how does man discover the God-concept—Thomas answers that man by inner drive is led to it inevitably, because the drive in man is to God, and the drive is in an agent who works through intelligence. Intelligence, therefore, will be pushed *a tergo* toward the investigation of God. Hence, for Thomas a natural theology is completely possible and inevitable in the human being we know. Given his suppositions, he has proved this to be so. No one has ever found a flaw in his arguments; all that has been done is to examine the arguments without the Thomistic suppositions, and the result of such an examination would be of no concern to Thomas. Concerning the suppositions, Thomas would only point out that they derive from an analysis of being, and that they are either *per se visa,* intuited immediately, or achieved by a further analysis of the original intuitions in terms of the laws of thought. That all men cannot see these suppositions, Thomas would admit as a contingent fact. He would, however, deny that this non-seeing derived from the physical incapacity of the intellect, affirming that such non-seeing was to be explained by the darkening effects of sin, a darkening which would never be complete.

9

The Limits of a Natural Theology

By the theodicy of Saint Thomas the mind achieves the Pure Act, the *Ens-a-se,* the Absolute. By his natural theology, this concept can be evolved into an infinite, eternal, omnipresent spirit, source and ground of all being. A spirit thinks and loves, and this we call personality, and so the Great Spirit is personal. However, all this structure is by way of negation and by way of analogy. We use essences in our description of the First Existent, but in him there is no essence, for his existence is his only essence.

Now it is evident that this kind of God is achieved as an object of thought. He is the *prius* of thinking, and thus the prius of being. God is not experienced. In experience, in existence, we cannot find him. Only through an analysis of thought down to its first implicit affirmation do we find the God of natural theology. He is a thought-absolute, but the God of religion as we know it is much richer than a thought-absolute. The study of natural theology produces no piety, no filial submission to a Father, no reverential fear of the Lord. Yet without such reactions there is no religion, at least as we know religion as an historical and psychological fact. A man may become enthusiastic for the magnificence of the mathematical method. Yet he will never become enthusiastic about the truth that the sum of all the angles of a triangle is equal to two right angles. You cannot pray to two right angles, nor can you pray to a Pure Act, nor to an *Ens-a-se*. The *devotus femineus sexus* would hardly get excited for a God so remote, so free from all the limitations of reality as it affects us in experience. The God of natural theology is all Logos.[1]

---

[1] *Logos* is Greek for thought, reason. *Eros* means love, as does *Agape*. *Agape* was especially applied to the love feast of the early Christians.

Eros has no part in him, but only in terms of Eros or Agape will man or woman act. Given man as he is, he morally needs some incarnation of the Logos, not necessarily as a human God, but at least as a God who speaks on Sinai, in the Burning Bush, in the Tent of the Covenant. God must be for men as they are today, not only logically, but also historically; not only behind history, but also in it.

If man as we know him had only a natural theology, he would not be religious, or better put, his religion would be restricted to his thought. His norm of behavior at very best would be the norm of reason, but not the will of God. He could ever say, "Thy will be done." This would seem to him silly, for the will of God could not be thwarted since it is equivalent to the necessitating drive in finite existence. Sin would not be a personal offense against God, and consequently no sin at all, but a mere mistake. There would be no propitiation for sin, but only remedial action against the unwanted effects of moral deficiency. There would be, as there was in Plotinus, the yogis, and the Buddhists, an irrational drive toward mystical experience, without knowing whether this was possible or not.

Natural theology could not give rise to a true cult of God. In cult, man tries to render aware his personal relationship with God. The supposition of all cult is that God is personally interested and concerned with me personally. The Logos of natural theology seems far removed from so human a phenomenon as concern. The only cult possible in a natural theology would be some pedagogic symbolism expressive of the recognition of Pure Act, the basis of all reality. It would be a philosophic pageant, but nothing more, and the vast majority of men who are cold to philosophy would like the pageant and ignore the philosophy.

It would seem just, therefore, to admit that natural theology is sterile as far as the erection of a religion is concerned. It can give a thought-absolute but it cannot give us a love-object with which we can become humanly involved.

Does this mean that natural theology is a chess game for philosophers and of no greater value for men? If all we know concerning God were to be derived from natural theology, it would not be highly valuable. However, that is not the human situation.

The one inescapable fact in human history is the all-pervading influence of religion on every age and in every place. One inescapable fact in this phenomenon is that the divine is always supposed to be breaking through historically. In dreams the American Indian established vital contact with the Spirit. The Great Spirit speaks to men. In the primitive cultures of Africa and the South Seas, the tribal god spoke to some of the ancients. His footprint is still seen on some stone; his mark is still visible in a tree or on a mountain side. In the gas-filled cave he can be heard, for the thunder of the volcano is the voice of God. Theophany is the universal note of all human religions. The grotesque attempts at forming a religion without theophany were so short-lived that we smile at the French Revolution putting the new goddess of Reason on the main altar of Notre Dame and we laugh heartily at Comte's religion of Positivism. Now can we do justice to the universal faith in theophanies by declaring smugly that the theophanies were imaginative interpretations of natural phenomena: the personification of the volcanic thunders and of the stormy sea. Moses did not confound the Burning Bush with God, nor did he personify the fire of the bush and thus call it Yahweh. In the Burning Bush Moses met something that was neither the fire nor the bush. Moses took his shoes off when he approached the bush, not because the bush was God, but because it was holy by reason of the theophanic presence of God. There was no intrinsic holiness in the bush. It was an extrinsic holiness poured over it by a personal God who spoke to Moses from the bush.

In other words, the history of mankind is evolved in terms of a supposition that God came to men in history. This is the revealing of God. According to *Genesis* the first human beings spoke to God frequently. They told their children about it. Every tradition contains other theophanies. A naturalist may say that all this is ancient ignorance and superstition, but not even the boldest naturalist can deny that the supposition of theophany is universal in the religious schemes of all cultures.

In other words, revelation is universally supposed in our history. In terms of such real or illusory revelations the religions of mankind were evolved. The great god Ra spoke to the Egyptians just as Yahweh spoke to the Israelites and later to the orthodox Christians in the man Jesus, who was the Son of God.

Saint Anselm and Saint Thomas listened to the words of Jesus, as they were delivered to them by the holy Church. These two saints had no desire to erect a religion or to construct a god. In terms of their faith, God simply was and is, and he showed man in an historical encounter the truth of God, which is normative for all men. The God of Anselm and Thomas was a living God, not a mere rational Logos. He was not a mental device to keep the spheres together and in motion. He was so real and all-but-tangible that Anselm breaks up the logical process of his thought in order to speak to him.

If this is so, why did Anselm and Thomas bother with a natural theology, which could give them so little? The answer is that they were men of intelligence, with a high regard for thought.

For Anselm it was self-evident that faith could only improve intelligence. It simply never occurred to him that anyone could think of faith as being opposed to intelligence. He loved both faith and reason with one single love. He realized that faith was not reason, but he could not understand that the two forms of knowledge could be at all divergent. Faith energizing intelligence could give to the latter form of knowledge a higher capacity and make it reach the heights of faith itself, which was for Anselm obviously superior to unaided intelligence. On the question of God, whom Anselm knew by faith, a corroborated intelligence could find much that was satisfying to a man who respects and loves intelligence. Hence, Anselm allowed his intelligence to deal with God, the only object he considered worthy of serious consideration, whether it was in terms of intelligence or faith.

Let us remember that Anselm's intelligence was not trying to discover God. He had discovered him already in faith. Anselm wanted to see what intelligence could offer to illuminate the discovery already made. Natural theology was, therefore, an enthusiastic act of faith. It was not a defense of anything, nor was it a means of quieting doubts, for Anselm did not doubt. For a believing philosophical thinker, natural theology will be the best loved branch of philosophy. By faith he enthusiastically affirms that the great reality is God, and that faith will move the believing philosopher to his task and faith will be the light which keeps him safely on the right road. The believing philosopher will not try to construct the God-concept but only rediscover by intelligence at least something of what he has already achieved by faith, not because faith needs reason, but because a believing intelligence cannot work except in terms of faith. The believer and the thinker are one, and faith commits the believer's intelligence to God-awareness.

Consequently, to a believing philosopher natural theology is not a chess game but an unavoidable examination. Aristotle taught that natural theology was the high point of philosophy. He had his reasons which were perhaps not wholly valid. The believer spontaneously agrees with Aristotle's doctrine for different reasons. By faith he is totally orientated to God, and in philosophy this orientation will inevitably drive him to the philosophic consideration of God, not as a means of discovery but rather as a service of faith. Only the believer who distrusts intelligence can object to such a service. Such a believer maintains that reason is ungodly. A Catholic believer could no more admit this than admit that there is no God. If God is, then reason is good and is a willing instrument of God. There need be no fear of it but rather a loving cultivation of its powers.

The Anselmic drive to natural theology is the true explanation of the importance of natural theology to a man who is fully aware that natural theology is not going to construct a religion. The task is not useless nor merely a precious exercise of method. It is the supreme philosophic task, and if philosophy is worthwhile, then *a fortiori,* natural theology is worthwhile.

In Thomas Aquinas we see a more complicated attitude to natural theology. Like Anselm, he recognized the primacy of faith over all forms of knowledge. Like Anselm, he considered the philosophic task honorable, useful, and precious. Consequently he believed that a natural theology was worthwhile. He too took his guidance from faith in his philosophic research but saw that such guidance was not necessary for philosophy in terms of its own method. Thomas recognized the limitations of philosophic method but he had enough confidence in it to think that, though it might lead to a question mark in certain problems, yet, if faithfully pursued, it would not lead to error. Gratefully he saw in his faith an extrinsic sure norm and valid inner dynamism for criticizing the validity of the philosophic findings of the intelligence which refused the orientation of faith. Thomas felt that he could show any philosopher who proposed doctrines contradictory to faith that the philosopher was using philosophic method badly and that his conclusions were fallacious. Thus for Thomas, natural theology was not only a labor of love on the part of the believing philosopher but also a weapon of defense of the Church in her jousts with the infidel. For Saint Thomas, natural theology had not only its intrinsic value, but also an extrinsic apologetic value.

Thomas had another insight. For him natural theology was necessary not only because it was the most appropriate task of the Catholic philosopher, not only because it was an apologetic weapon for the Church against her adversaries, but it was also necessary in order that the Catholic intellectual be rationally justified. As a philosopher, the Catholic philosopher was committed to the proposition that all reality was intelligible, either because its intrinsic intelligibility could be achieved, or at least its reasonableness could be recognized. Faith itself was a reality and therefore it must be shown as intelligible or at least reasonable. Faith rested on the word of God. Hence, God must somehow be known with logical priority before his word can be accepted. Therefore before faith —before, that is, in logic though not necessarily in time—the existence of God must be proved. If God is not, there can be no word of God.

God must be achieved before his word can be known. Hence, the Catholic philosopher is forced by philosophy and not merely by faith to investigate first of all the reality of God, for otherwise faith will not be a reasonable state, and if it is not a reasonable state, then it cannot guide the philosopher even extrinsically.

Now Saint Thomas was fully aware that philosophic reasoning could not give him the fullness of the living God. The final conclusions of the Five Ways in the *Summa* always have the same wording: "And this is what men understand by God"; "And this is what men call God." Perhaps these words can be more pertinently proposed in the following formula: "And our concept of God can be partially expressed in terms of First Mover, Ultimate Cause, Pure Act, Perfect Being, World Governor." He is not saying that the concept of God is limited to such terms; the limited conceptions of philosophy find their object in the God that Thomas had met in faith. Reason points to the God of faith; it cannot adequately express him. The pointers are clear enough to make the act of faith reasonable, though they are not enough to make God perfectly transparent. In this way natural theology was for Thomas the first duty of the Catholic philosopher. As a philosopher he had to show that it was reasonable to be guided by faith and as a Catholic he had to deal with God in whom he believed.

This attitude to natural theology avoids two extremes in our times. Many Catholics who deal with natural theology seem to be too interested in theodicy as an apologetic weapon. Their aim is to persuade. Persuasion is not the same as proof and proof is not the same as persuasion. Persuasion is possible where there is no proof and proof is possible where there is no persuasion. In fact, the strongest abstract proofs usually have but small persuasive value for the man of "common sense."

In the same manner, many Catholics identify the Catholic concept of God, so rich and so variegated, with the God of natural theology, who is only a thought-absolute. The two *conceptions* by no legitimate title are identical or coterminous. The *object* of both conceptions is identical but the conceptions are quite distinct. The Catholic is unwittingly filling out the meager natural theology conceptions with all the wealth of his faith commitments. He is then surprised that the non-believer will give only a limited recognition to the natural theology conceptions but will not admit the Catholic God. The Catholic either becomes puzzled or indignant. When he stays in a puzzled mood, he begins to doubt the validity of his philosophic method and he can become skeptical with regard to the validity of philosophy. When he is indignant, he accuses his debating adversary of willfulness and lack of sincerity.

Both of these reactions are unjustified. There is no need to become skeptical of reason because its proofs do not persuade. This is not the function of philosophy, nor of proof. Above all, the Catholic should see that his proofs have not been altogether rejected. They have been accepted in the form of idolatry, since the non-believer has no choice but to construct his god and god-construction is idolatry. Natural theology points inexorably to the Unknown God of whom St. Paul spoke on the Areopagus,[2] but he, as a living God, still remains unknown and the human spirit will not tolerate this void of knowing. A man will fill it with the things he knows best, making a god with the stuff of time and space, and that is idolatry. It is literally true that only the madman can say there is no God, for thinking requires its absolute to which every thinker must submit, and only unreason will not admit it. However, the mere admission does not mean that man has reached the living God. Man can tamper with his intuitions and render them corrupt. This he has done over and over again in the long history of humanity. The classical cultures made the powers in nature divine—sky-god, sun-god, moon-god. The same cultures made human energies divine—fecundity-gods, vene-real-gods. This is happening again in our day. Einstein believes in the divinity of the total universe, this vast energy system. His Jewish fore-fathers would have cried: "Idolatry!" and they would have been quite right. Freud found the absolute in the sex-drive in man. Again his Jewish forefathers would have branded him as an idolater. There is no difference between Jupiter-Zeus and the Einsteinian god, just as there is no differ-ence between Venus-Astarte and the Freudian basic drive in man. The ancient parallelism is even more visible in Karl Marx, for like his ancient progenitors, he made the golden calf the god of salvation. The Einstein-Freud-Marx mythologies are different from those of the olden time, but in intent they are unchanged. They are idolaters, not because they deny the divine, but because they refuse to recognize that Yahweh alone is God. Now Yahweh is not met as Yahweh in reason. He is met in faith. Hence, the Catholic must not be surprised that his arguments which point to God inexorably yet do not show us the veiled face of Yahweh. The showing of himself is a task that can be accomplished by Yahweh alone. Like Paul, the Catholic must explain to the jeering sophisticates that we know the Unknown God, but neither Paul nor the modern Catholic can make his hearer see it. If the hearer is culturally condi-tioned against faith, it will be difficult for him to see, and only the sana-tive breath of God can facilitate the task for him. Reason has not failed; it keeps its everlasting power. Men have failed, as they always have failed,

---

[2] *Acts* 17, 23-24.

to be led by reason, because their minds are darkened by the ancient sin which still abides with us.

If despair caused by the lack of persuasiveness in the philosophic proof of the existence of God is not justified, indignation is even less so. Tillich has said that many an atheist is a firmer believer in God than some religious people. What he means is that the atheist has implicitly so refined a notion of divinity that he will not accept idolatrous substitutes for it. Be that as it may, it is true that many non-believers became so because the communication of revelation to them was in very earthy terms. God was the old white-bearded man clad in many-folded sheets sitting on a cloud and looking sternly down on the earth. The non-believer took this description quite literally and believed that the men of religion took it quite literally. In that hypothesis, a knowledge of God would make him reject the old-man-god and make him look for God elsewhere. It is an interesting fact that the early Christians, who were certainly God-conscious far beyond their pagan fellows, were sincerely accused of atheism. Their atheism consisted in rejecting the idols of their time as diabolical caricatures of God. They refused to drop a pinch of incense on the altar of Mars, not because they refused to adore God, but because they refused to insult God by admitting that the martial spirit was the ground of being, the living God. They were instead quite willing to give witness to the existence of the real God in the highest form of witness for a human being, and they used the word "witness" for the great act—martyrdom, which literally means "bearing witness."

The martyr did not attempt to show the living God to the pagan with the arguments of natural theology. He knew that natural theology could not do that, valid and efficacious as it was for something less. The Christian martyr was not indignant with his pagan compatriots. Instead, in an act of great love he gave witness to the reality of the living God in such a way that the pagan had to be impressed, and therefore Tertullian was quite right when he said that the blood of the martyrs was the seed of the Church. Persuasion does not come from Logos; it comes from Agape. Because the Christian loved God and loved his neighbor, he was ready, and in some cases anxious, to give the highest witness to God whom the martyr loved, to his fellowmen whom the martyr also loved. If I tell you that I met John Jones in Jersey City, you are faced with an existential fact which cannot be derived from mere reasoning. If I am ready to die for my affirmation, that is the strongest way I can insist on the experience I had, and you are led to the simplest conclusion: He did see something in Jersey City. My witness forces you to examine my statement as nothing else can.

The persuasion of the neighbor is not a Logos task. It is the task of Eros. Yet it must be the high Eros, which the Christians call Agape. I do not persuade the neighbor of God's existence so that he makes my group stronger in the world and thus makes me greater. Such an act is neither the love of God nor the love of the neighbor. It is putting the religion of the Living God at the service of idolatry. Let our persuasion be that of the witness, the witness in the hand of God, whom God uses for his designs. If God's design for a human soul is to bring it to the knowledge of the Living God, besides the use of human witnesses, he will also give testimony of himself within the human soul he is seeking. Without that inner testimony, the external witnessing cannot be effective.

10

Conclusions

From our conception of religion we declared that the center of religion was the numinous, God. We have examined the philosophic approaches to God. We have found that the philosophers have found God in a number of ways, which for practical purposes we can reduce to eleven.

Of these eleven, we found only seven truly philosophic, and of these seven we found only five properly formulated according to the laws of philosophic method.

Of these five we could say that they were different expressions of one basic philosophic principle: the relative is unthinkable, and thus unrealizable, unless there is logically prior to it an absolute. This principle must be used in the existential order, because if it is used only of the essential, we derive no right to speak of God as existent. God is not a mathematical object.

The existent as relative can be seen in five ways: the empirical objects change; empirical being is caused; empirical being is marked by change and causation as contingent; empirical being which is contingent is recognized as imperfect; empirical being is a unity composed of self-adjusting plurality relative to that unity.

Hence, on principle, philosophy necessarily leads to the Absolute, but the epistemological presuppositions are: (1) knowledge, metaphysical or empirical, achieves the real in itself; (2) reality is an analogous term. This analogy is primarily evident in the real distinction between essence and existence, giving to existence the necessary primacy because it is the source of being, which can be shared. Without these presuppositions the conceptual proofs cannot operate. These suppositions are not *fiat* postulates but the inevitable conclusions of the analysis of knowledge. They are intuited, *per se visa,* in their core.

To the question—is God existentially real—philosophy answers affirmatively.

There is a prior question: How did the philosopher get the God-concept at all? To this question we have the following answers:

(1) De facto, religion which is a cultural phenomenon around the God-concept, is an all pervasive fact and religion, as we know it, supposes that God revealed himself to men. If this supposition is valid, then philosophers ultimately achieve the God-concept from a human experience of God.

(2) Given the validity of the God-concept, it is clear that man's drive, which is the center of his being and action, is a drive to God. Although a drive can be blind, yet a reflection on the drive will suggest spontaneously the God-concept whose validity must be established by arguments other than the mere fact of basic drive. Only in this way can we admit any innate knowledge of God; it is innate unconscious knowledge, which can be rendered conscious by metaphysical reasoning.

Concerning the limitations of the religion of metaphysics, we said that the God-concept of natural theology would not found religion as we know it and as it is effective for man. A metaphysical religion is not a true religion which embraces the total man in terms of relationship to a living God. For such a religion, revelation is necessary. The God of metaphysics could found something like religion as we know it, but it would be thin, intellectual, and not very effective. Yet natural theology is not useless, because it can be employed in revealed religion as the rational guarantee for the validity of an approach to God through revelation.

Hence, to the possible answers which we proposed to the question of the philosophical approach to God and which we indicated as four— (1) Metaphysics can rationally justify the religious experience, without delimiting precisely the content of religion. (2) Metaphysics can deduce an adequate religious scheme. (3) Metaphysics refutes the religious claims. (4) Metaphysics has nothing to say about religion.—we can answer by rejecting three of the logically possible answers. Metaphysics has something to say about the religious enterprise. It certainly does not refute the claims of religion. It justifies religion inadequately and cannot produce an adequate religion by its own power alone.

Selected
Bibliography
for Part I

On Religion as a Phenomenon and Religious Knowledge

Bennett, Charles A., *The Dilemma of Religious Knowledge*. New Haven: Yale University Press, 1931.

Brightman, Edgar S., *A Philosophy of Religion*. Englewood Cliffs, N.J.: Prentice-Hall, Inc., 1940.

Bronstein, D. J., *et al.*, *Basic Problems of Philosophy*. Englewood Cliffs, N.J.: Prentice-Hall, 1955.

D'Arcy, M. C., *The Nature of Belief*. New York: Sheed & Ward, 1945.

Dewey, John, *A Common Faith*. New Haven, Conn.: Yale University Press, 1934.

James, William, *The Varieties of Religious Experience*. New York: Longmans, Green & Company, 1902 (many reprints).

Kaufman, Gordon D., *Relativism, Knowledge and Faith*. Chicago: University of Chicago Press, 1960.

Knudson, Albert C., *Basic Issues in Christian Thought*. New York: Abingdon-Cokesbury, 1950.

Macgregor, Geddes, *Introduction to Religious Philosophy*. Boston: Houghton Mifflin Company, 1959.

Macintosh, Douglas C., *The Problems of Religious Knowledge*. New York: Harper & Brothers, 1940.

Martineau, James, *A Study of Religion, Its Sources and Contents*, 2nd ed., rev. Oxford: The Clarendon Press, 1900.

Otto, Rudolf, *The Idea of the Holy*, 4th impression, revised with additions, trans. J. W. Harvey. London: H. Milford, Oxford University Press, 1926.

Pratt, James Bissett, *The Religious Consciousness*. New York: The Macmillan Company, 1937.

Radin, Paul, *Primitive Religion*. New York: Dover Publications, Inc., 1957.

Randall, John Herman, Jr., *The Role of Knowledge in Western Religion*. Boston: Starr King Press, 1958.

Royce, Josiah, *The Sources of Religious Insight*. New York: Charles Scribner's Sons, 1912.

166 BIBLIOGRAPHY

Thompson, Samuel, *A Modern Philosophy of Religion*. Chicago: Henry Regnery Company, 1955.
Thomte, Reidar, *Kierkegaard's Philosophy of Religion*. Princeton, N.J.: Princeton University Press, 1948.
Tillich, Paul, *The Protestant Era*. Chicago: University of Chicago Press, 1948.

Psychology and Religion

Allport, Gordon W., *The Individual and His Religion*. New York: The Macmillan Company, 1950.
Boeuf, Marie (pseud. Camille Bos) , *Psychologie de la Croyance*. Paris: F. Alcan, 1901.
Coe, George Albert, *The Psychology of Religion*. Chicago: University of Chicago Press, 1916.
Conklin, Edmund S., *The Psychology of Religious Adjustment*. New York: The Macmillan Company, 1929.
Dunlap, Knight, *Religion: Its Functions in Human Life*. New York: McGraw-Hill Book Company, Inc., 1946.
Fromm, Erich, *Psychoanalysis and Religion*. New Haven, Conn.: Yale University Press, 1950.
Hadfield, J. A., *Psychology and Morals*. New York: R. M. McBride & Company, 1923.
Inge, William Ralph, *Faith and its Psychology*. New York: Charles Scribner's Sons, 1910.
Jung, Carl Gustav, *Psychology and Religion*. New Haven, Conn.: Yale University Press, 1938; paperback edition, 1960.
Leuba, James, *A Psychological Study of Religion*. New York: The Macmillan Company, 1912.
Oliver, John Rathbone, *Psychiatry and Mental Health*. New York: Charles Scribner's Sons, 1932.
Pratt, James Bissett, *The Psychology of Religious Belief*. New York: The Macmillan Company, 1907.
Starbuck, Edwin Diller, *The Psychology of Religion,* 3rd ed. New York: Charles Scribner's Sons, 1911.
Stratton, G. M., *Psychology of the Religious Life*. New York: The Macmillan Company, 1918.
Thouless, Robert H., *An Introduction to the Psychology of Religion*. Cambridge: The University Press, 1936.
Weigel, Gustave, *Psicología de la Religión*. Santiago de Chile: Editorial Difusión Chilena, 1945.

Mysticism

Bennett, Charles A., *A Philosophical Study of Mysticism*. New Haven, Conn.: Yale University Press, 1923.
von Hügel, Baron Friedrich, *The Mystical Element of Religion as Studied in*

Saint Catherine of Genoa and Her Friends, 2nd ed. New York: E. P. Dutton & Company, 1923.

Leuba, James, *The Psychology of Religious Mysticism.* New York: Harcourt Brace & Company, 1925.

Maréchal, Joseph, *Studies in the Psychology of the Mystics,* trans. Algar Thorold. London: Burns, Oates and Washbourne, 1927.

Récéjac, E., *The Bases of the Mystical Knowledge,* trans. S. C. Upton. New York: Charles Scribner's Sons, 1899.

Saint Teresa of Jesus, *Complete Works,* 3 vols., ed. E. Allison Peers. New York: Sheed & Ward, 1946.

Underhill, Evelyn, *The Essentials of Mysticism.* London: J. M. Dent & Sons, 1920.

————, *Mysticism. A Study in the Nature and Development of Man's Spiritual Consciousness.* New York: Meridian Books, 1956.

Zaehner, R. C., *Mysticism Sacred and Profane.* Oxford at Clarendon Press, 1957.

Selected
Bibliography
for Part II

Natural Theology from Plato to Kant

Plato, *The Laws*, Bk. X, 885b-907; *Timaeus*, 27b-69, in *The Dialogues of Plato*, 4 vols., 4th ed., ed. Benjamin Jowett. New York: Oxford University Press, 1953.

More, Paul Elmer, *The Religion of Plato*, 2nd ed. rev. Princeton, N.J.: Princeton University Press, 1928.

Aristotle, *Metaphysics*, Bk. I and Bk. XII, in *The Works of Aristotle: The Oxford Translation*, ed. J. A. Smith and W. D. Ross, 12 vols. London and New York: Oxford University Press, 1910-1952.

Lucretius, *On the Nature of Things*, trans. Cyril Bailey. Oxford: The Clarendon Press, 1910.

Cicero, *De Natura Deorum; Academica*, with an English translation by H. Rackham (Loeb Classical Library). London: W. Heinemann, Ltd., 1933.

Epictetus, *Discourses and Enchiridion*, based on the translation of T. W. Higginson. New York: Published for the Classics Club by W. J. Black, 1944.

Marcus Aurelius Antoninus, *The Meditations of Marcus Aurelius* (Everyman's Library). New York: E. P. Dutton & Company, 1935.

Plotinus, *The Enneads*, trans. Stephen MacKenna, 2nd ed. rev. by B. S. Page. New York: Pantheon Books, Inc., 1957.

Whittaker, Thomas, *The Neo-Platonists*. Cambridge: Cambridge University Press, 1928.

Pseudo-Dionysius, *De Divinis Nominibus* (Christian Neo-Platonism). Migne's *Patrologia Graeca*, Vol. 3.

Saint Augustine, *De Trinitate*. Migne's *Patrologia Latina*, Vol. 42.

Saint Anselm of Canterbury, *Monologium, Proslogium* and the controversy with Gaunilo. Migne's *Patrologia Latina*, Vol. 158. For a translation of these see St. Anselm, *Proslogium; Monologium; An Appendix in behalf of the Fool by Gaunilon; and Cur Deus Homo*, trans. S. N. Deane. La Salle, Ill.: Open Court Publishing Company, 1958.

Barth, Karl, *Fides Quaerens Intellectum, Forschungen zur Geschichte und Lehre des Protestantismus*, 4te Reihe, 3 Bd. Munich: Chr. Kaiser Verlag, 1931. There is an English translation by Ian W. Robertson, published under the title *Anselm: Fides Quaerens Intellectum*. Richmond, Va.: John Knox Press, 1960.

Saint Thomas Aquinas, *Summa contra Gentiles*, trans. Fathers of the English Dominican Province. New York: Benziger Brothers, 1923-1929.

————, *Summa Theologica*, Part I, in *Basic Writings of St. Thomas Aquinas*, ed. Anton C. Pegis, 2 vols. New York: Random House, Inc., 1945.

Dowey, Edward A., Jr., *The Knowledge of God in Calvin's Theology*. New York: Columbia University Press, 1952.

Descartes, René, *Discourse on Method, Meditations on the First Philosophy and Principles of Philosophy*, trans. J. Veitch, Everyman's Library, American edition. New York: E. P. Dutton & Company, 1951.

Spinoza, Baruch (Benedict), *The Ethics*, Part I, Concerning God, in Vol. II of *The Chief Works of Benedict de Spinoza*, trans. R. H. M. Elwes. New York: Dover Publications, Inc., 1951.

Leibnitz, Gottfried Wilhelm, *Theodicy*, trans. E. M. Haggard. London: Routledge & Kegan Paul, 1952.

Kant, Immanuel, *Critique of Pure Reason*, trans. F. Max Müller. New York: The Macmillan Company, 2nd ed. rev., 1934.

England, F. E., *Kant's Conception of God*. London: G. Allen and Unwin, Ltd., 1929.

Catholic Manuals of Natural Theology

Boedder, Bernard, *Natural Theology*, 2nd ed. New York: Longmans, Green & Company, 1921.

Garrigou-Lagrange, Reginald, *God: His Existence and His Nature*, 2 vols. Saint Louis: B. Herder Book Company, 1934-1936.

Gilson, Etienne, *Elements of Christian Philosophy*. Garden City, N. Y., Doubleday & Company, 1960.

Hawkins, D. J. B., *The Essentials of Theism*. New York: Sheed & Ward, 1950.

Holloway, Maurice E., *An Introduction to Natural Theology*, New York: Appleton-Century-Crofts, Inc., 1959.

McCormick, John, *Natural Theology*. Chicago: Loyola University Press, 1943.

Mercier, Desiré Cardinal, *A Manual of Modern Scholastic Philosophy*, trans. T. L. and S. A. Parker, 3rd ed. Saint Louis: B. Herder Book Company, 1932.

de Raeymaeker, Louis, *The Philosophy of Being*. Saint Louis: B. Herder Book Company, 1954.

Rickaby, Joseph, *Studies on God and His Creatures*. London: Longmans, Green & Company, 1924.

Sheen, Fulton, *God and Intelligence in Modern Philosophy*. New York: Longmans, Green & Company, 1925.

————, *Religion without God*. New York: Longmans, Green & Company, 1928.

Smith, Gerard, *Natural Theology*. New York: The Macmillan Company, 1951.

Modern Approaches

Pragmatism

James, William, *The Varieties of Religious Experience*. New York: Longmans, Green & Company, 1902 (many reprints).

Psychoanalysis

Fromm, Erich, *Psychoanalysis and Religion*. New Haven, Conn.: Yale University Press, 1950.
Zilboorg, Gregory, *Mind, Medicine and Man*. New York: Harcourt, Brace & Company, 1943.

Positivism and Analysis

Charlesworth, M. J., "Linguistic Analysis and Language about God" in *International Philosophical Quarterly*, Vol. I, no. 1 (February 1961), pp. 139-167.
Collins, James, "Analytic Theism and Demonstrative Inference" in *International Philosophical Quarterly*, Vol. I, no 2 (May 1961), pp. 235-263.
Feigel, H. and W. Sellars, *Readings in Philosophic Analysis*. New York: Appleton-Century-Crofts, Inc., 1949.
Flew, A. and Macintyre, A., eds., *New Essays in Philosophical Theology*. New York: The Macmillan Company, 1955.
von Mises, Richard, *Positivism*. Cambridge, Mass.: Harvard University Press, 1951.
Wisdom, John, "Gods" in *Essays in Logic and Language,* ed. Antony Flew. New York: Philosophical Library, 1951.

Existentialism

Atheistic

Sartre, Jean-Paul, *Being and Nothingness,* Part III, trans. H. E. Barnes. New York: Philosophical Library, 1956.
————, *Existentialism and Human Emotions*. New York: Philosophical Library, 1957.
Collins, James, *The Existentialists*. Chicago: Henry Regnery Company, 1952.

Non-atheistic

Jaspers, Karl, *The Perennial Scope of Philosophy,* trans. Ralph Manheim. New York: Philosophical Library, 1949.

Protestant Theological Existentialism

Barth, Karl, *Die Christliche Dogmatik,* Bd. I, *Die Lehre vom Worte Gottes.* Munich: Chr. Kaiser Verlag, 1927. English translation: *The Doctrine of the Word of God,* trans. G. Thomson. Edinburgh: T. & T. Clark, 1936.

Brunner, Emil, *Dogmatics,* I, *The Christian Doctrine of God,* trans. Olive Wyon. Philadelphia: Westminster Press, 1952.

————, *The Divine-Human Encounter,* trans. Amandus Loos. Philadelphia: Westminster Press, 1943.

Tillich, Paul, *Systematic Theology.* Chicago: University of Chicago Press, Vol. I, 1951; Vol. II, 1957.

De Wolf, L. Harold, *Religious Revolt against Reason.* New York: Harper & Brothers, 1949.

Macquarrie, John, *Existentialist Theology.* New York: The Macmillan Company, 1955.

Weigel, Gustave, "The Theological Significance of Paul Tillich." *Gregorianum,* Vol. XXXVII, no. 1, 1956; also in *Cross Currents,* Vol. VI, no. 2 (Spring 1956).

Jewish Existentialism

Herberg, Will, *Judaism and Modern Man.* New York: Farrar, Strauss & Young, 1951.

Catholic Criticism of Existentialism

Pius XII, *Humani Generis,* August 12, 1950, AAS 42 (1950) 561-78.

Protestant Liberal Theology

Bennett, Charles A., *The Dilemma of Religious Knowledge.* New Haven, Conn.: Yale University Press, 1931.

Wieman, Harry N., *The Wrestle of Religion with Truth.* New York: The Macmillan Company, 1927.

Protestant Empirical Theology

Bertocci, Peter Anthony, *Introduction to the Philosophy of Religion.* Englewood Cliffs, N. J.: Prentice-Hall, Inc., 1951.

Brightman, Edgar S., *A Philosophy of Religion.* Englewood Cliffs, N.J.: Prentice-Hall, Inc., 1940.

Protestant Fundamentalist Theology

Carnell, Edward John, *The Case for Orthodox Theology.* Philadelphia: Westminster Press, 1959.

Henry, Carl F. H., *The Drift of Western Thought.* Grand Rapids, Mich.: Wm. B. Eerdmans Publishing Company, 1951.

Catholic Critical Approach

Collins, James, *God in Modern Philosophy*. Chicago: Henry Regnery Company, 1959.

Danielou, Jean, *God and the Ways of Knowing*. New York: Meridian Books, Inc., 1957.

Dumery, Henry, *Le Probleme de Dieu*. Bruges (Belgique): Desclée de Brouwer, 1956.

de Lubac, Henri, *Discovery of God*, trans. Alexander Dru. New York: P. J. Kenedy & Sons, 1960.

Maritain, Jacques, *Approaches to God*. New York: Harper & Brothers, 1954.

Other Pertinent Works

Casserley, J. V. Langmead, *The Christian in Philosophy*. New York: Charles Scribner's Sons, 1951.

————, *Graceful Reason, the Contribution of Reason to Theology*. Greenwich, Conn.: Seabury Press, 1954.

Ferre, Nels F. S., *Faith and Reason*. New York: Harper & Brothers, 1946.

Frank, Erich, *Philosophical Understanding and Religious Truth*. New York: Oxford University Press, 1945.

Heschel, Abraham J., *God in Search of Man, a Philosophy of Judaism*. New York: Farrar, Strauss & Cudahy, 1955.

Hutchison, John A., *Faith, Reason and Existence, an Introduction to Contemporary Philosophy of Religion*. New York: Oxford University Press, 1956.

Kaufmann, Walter, *Critique of Religion and Philosophy*. New York: Harper & Brothers, 1958.

Lewis, H. D., *Our Experience of God*. London: G. Allen & Unwin, Ltd., 1959.

Mascall, E. L., *Existence and Analogy*. New York: Longmans, Green & Company, 1949.

————, *He Who Is, a Study in Traditional Theism*. New York: Longmans, Green & Company, 1954.

Weigel, Gustave, "Paul Tillich and Contemporaneous Protestantism" in *Theological Studies*, Vol. XI, 1950, pp. 547-556.

————, *A Survey of Protestant Theology in Our Day*. Westminster, Md.: Newman Press, 1954.

Weiss, Paul, *Modes of Being*. Carbondale, Ill.: Southern Illinois University Press, 1958.

Index of Topics

Absolute:

intuition of, 14; all reality related to, 16; relative demands, existence of, 18; man may reason to, 21; numen as a philosophical, 24-25; discovery in philosophy, 28; philosophical absolute not the object of prayer, 82; admission of finite being commits one to recognition of, 132; relative implies, 144; mind achieves the, 154; thinking requires its, 160; relative unthinkable without an, 163

Adolescence:

conversion in, 60-61; gregariousness in, 65-66

Agape, 154-155, 161

Agnosticism, 125

Allah, 9

Analogy:

of concepts applied to numinous, 17; of being, 25; excursus on, 28-31; valid construction of numinous in terms of, 86; knowledge of God possible by, 128; evident in real distinction between essence and existence, 163

Ancestor worship, Chinese, 3

Anglicanism:

the Mass in, 52; marriage a sacrament in, 63

Animism:

not necessarily religious, 1, 2, 3; in primitive cultures, 6, 12

Anti-clericalism, 40

A posteriori:

argument for existence of God, 124; Leibniz's notion of, 135; first three of "Five Ways," 144

A priori:

answers to why men assent to numinous, 8; denial of mystical encounter, 71-72; denial that God can reveal himself, 87; logic can proceed, 124; Descartes worked, 130; Leibniz's notion of, 135; reason in Kant, 136, 137

Asceticism, 13, 48, 73

Assent, prudential, 89

Atheism (Atheists):

answer to the reality of the numinous, 10-11; Tillich's claim that there are no, 15; sentiment secures religion against attacks of, 50; not "natural," 59; not systematically taught or defended in 2nd century A.D., 108; Kant anxious to save religion from attacks of, 136; more congenial to positivism than a theistic vision, 141; Tillich maintains many are firm believers in God, 161

Attributes, divine, 129, 131-132, 154

Auto-suggestion, 35

Beatific Vision, 73

Beatitude, 124

Being-as-such, 14, 29, 31

Brahmanism, 1

Break-through into history, divine:

epistemology should not deny possibility of, 88-92; one of seven arguments considered by St. Thomas, 144; universality of belief in, 155-156

Buddhism:

is it a religion?, 1; goal of asceticism of, 13; rosary in, 56-57; celibacy in, 63; mystical tradition in, 68; irrational drive to mystical experience in, 155

Calvinism, 46-47

Cartesianism, 130-134

Categories:

numinous is beyond our, 6, 8, 13, 15; only instruments for knowing God, 17; "is" is not a category, 30; cannot limit the absolute, 83; denied of God, 128; considered a human construction by nominalists, 129

Catholicism (Catholics, Catholic belief):

Reformers replaced numinal scheme of,

173

Scientific method, 9, 140, 147
Scriptures:
the vehicle of revelation for Protestants, 24; contains erotic poems, 61; gave no philosophic support to Jewish religion, 105; Abelard and, 119; dogmas of faith depend on, 121; Calvin and, 130; miraculous one of the principal contents of, 134; existentialist theologians and the, 142
Self-conservation, 58-59
Semantics, 113, 141
Sentiment, religion as, 4
Sermon meeting, 51-52
Sex experience, 3
Sex instinct, 59-65
Sex love, 62
Shakers, 63
Shinto, 1
Sin, 48-49, 155
Sophists, 43, 101
Sosein, 29, 30, 83
Spiritual Nuptials, 76-77
Spiritualism, 3
Stoicism:
modified classical religious framework, 6; natural theology of, 103-104; Jewish influence in creation of, 105; was a materialism, 108; "second way" of St. Thomas had been proposed by, 143
Summa contra Gentiles of St. Thomas, 121-126, 127, 128, 131
Summa Theologica of St. Thomas, 17, 121, 126-129, 143-144
Supernatural, 90
Suggestion:
explanation of, 34-42; resistance to, 36; and the assent to the numinous, 38-40; limits of, 40; validity of, 41-42; prayer as, 58; mystical phenomena said to be products of, 70

Tabu, 46
Theology as intellectual discipline of religion, 79-81
Theophany:
among primitive peoples, 12-13; among Hebrews, 14; in St. Paul, 106-107; universal in all religions, 156
Thing-in-itself, 85-86, 136
Theodicy (natural theology):
found in Catholicism and Protestantism, 18; William James' opposition to, 18;

does not give numinous as numinous, 86, 87; intentions of this study of, 95-96; Epictetus outlines a, 104; Pauline, 105-107; in the Fathers of the Church, 109; early medievalists needed no, 110; Peter Lombard's, 120-121; in the *contra Gentiles,* 121 ff.; Thomas' dependence on Aristotle for starting point in, 129; later Lutheran theologians developed a, 130; Descartes', 130-131; Leibniz's, 132-134; Kant's treatment of, 136 ff.; existentialist theologians foes of, 142; St. Thomas believes it possible, 153; limits of, 154-162

Union with God, 47-49

Values:
religion as a pursuit of, 9; God reduced to finite, 27-28
Vatican Council, 17, 142
Vestal virgins, 62
Via remotionis, 128
Voluntarism:
of Paul Tillich, 15-17; strength and weakness of, 18-19; Catholicism does not overlook facts stressed by, 25-27; denies intellect's capacity to achieve the real, 27; continental positivism voluntaristic, 141

Yahweh:
known by Hebrews through revelation, 14; thunders on Sinai, 45; met by Moses in personal encounter, 68; intensely personal Hebrew God, 101; revealed himself in nature to gentiles according to St. Paul, 106; Moses did not confound the Burning Bush with, 156; spoke to Israelites, 156; idolaters refuse to recognize that Yahweh alone is God, 160
Yoga:
goal is to see numinous face to face, 13; posture and position important in, 39; breathing technique of, 55; celibacy in, 63; mystical contemplation in, 68; asceticism in, 73; drive toward mystical experience in, 155

Zeus, 104

Index of Names